ECO-LITERACY FOR PRIMARY SCHOOLS

ECO-LITERACY FOR PRIMARY SCHOOLS

Alan Peacock

Trentham Books

Stoke on Trent, UK and Sterling, USA

Trentham Books Limited

Westview House	22883 Quicksilver Drive
734 London Road	Sterling
Oakhill	VA 20166-2012
Stoke on Trent	USA
Staffordshire	
England ST4 5NP	

First published 2004

British Library Cataloguing-in-Publication Data
A catalogue record for this book is available from the
British Library

1 85856 304 6

*Illustrations on pages 23, 30, 46, 51, 53, 54, 55, 81, 82, 84, 87
by Dai Owen*

Designed and typeset by Trentham Print Design Ltd., Chester and printed in Great Britain by Cromwell Press Ltd, Wiltshire.

Contents

To Jill and her team at Carymoor Environmental Centre
and to Jo and her team at the Eden Project

Acknowledgements

Trying to break new ground in primary teaching and learning always requires support and trust, and I owe a lot to people who gave me confidence during the conception and writing of this book. The original inspiration came from the books and personal enthusiasms of Fritjof Capra, Joseph Cornell and the late Sir Alec Clegg. Ideas, activities and approaches often emanated from (or were bounced off) colleagues and students, including Rob Bowker, Beth Gompertz and the Primary PGCE students at Exeter University; Nick Pratt and Alan Dyer at Plymouth University; John Parry at Sussex University; Mark Rickinson of the NFER's Environmental Research Network; and Cathy Burke at Leeds University, who all provided fascinating insights into children's and teachers' ideas.

I also owe a great deal to two enterprises that embody the philosophy of this book. Firstly, to the education team at the Eden Project, especially the support and enthusiasm of Jo Readman, Gill Hodgson, Pam Horton and Andy Jasper. Secondly, to the staff of Carymoor Environmental Centre, particularly Jill Vrdlovcova the Executive Director, and the Somerset Waste Action Programme headed by Rupert Farthing. I also need to thank Wyvern Waste, the company managing the landfill site at Carymoor, for use of some photographs and for their forward-looking approach to education about waste minimisation which, along with the impressive resource support of Somerset County and District Councils, has helped the Carymoor team create an education facility second to none. Finally, I have learned a great deal from recently evaluating the National Trust/Norwich Union Guardianship Scheme: my thanks go to Alison Lipscombe and all the wardens around the country who do such exciting work with children out of school. It has been an immense pleasure to work with such dedicated teams over the past three years.

In putting together the book, I also owe thanks to Gillian Klein, for her commitment to the original idea and to her immaculate editing; to John Stipling, for his patience and advice in reproducing a wide variety of artwork; and to my own children Laurent (for designing several diagrams) and Katie, for her careful proof-reading of the final manuscript. After reading this book, teachers and others will no doubt contest and argue about the ideas and approaches it embodies; and this for me is a positive thing. I see this book as an attempt to raise the profile of eco-thinking in schools: may there be many more on this vital theme in children's future learning.

1

What this book is for

This book is one outcome of many years working with primary teachers and trainees who are concerned about what is happening to the world we live in and want to address these concerns with children. So it is a book about the basic facts of life in the early 21st century. It is not a scary, doom-and-gloom book. Its purpose is to help you feel more confident in dealing with complex concepts such as ecology, bio-diversity and sustainability – the new 'facts of life' – in a way that children will find interesting and relevant. Hopefully, it will excite you and persuade you to put more emphasis on these vital issues in your work with children.

It is also a book about the need for vision. Watching TV programmes such as 'Changing Rooms' reminds me that you can't begin to redecorate until you have a vision of what you want the room to look like. This applies on a much bigger scale: we can't help children to think and learn and live in new ways unless we, their parents and teachers, have a clear vision of what it is that matters.

The book starts by helping you think about the idea of eco-literacy, by breaking it down into simpler ideas. One big idea here is that our lives, our small planet and all our actions are interlinked through networks. This is true of animals and plants, as well as our communities, businesses, technologies, oceans, weather and global politics. We grow corn to feed cattle, sell the meat to Europe and import just as much meat back: why? What would happen if all the bees that pollinate plants were killed off? These are questions children might ask: they are questions about the Web of Life. First, here are some of the key words:

Some key eco-words and their meanings

ECO-
From the Greek *OIKOS*, a house

ECOLOGY
The relation of organisms to one another and to their physical environment

ECOSYSTEM
A unit of organisms and their habitat (e.g. a rainforest, a pond)

ECONOMY
From the Greek *OIKONOMOS*, a manager of a household, or steward

Hence the links:

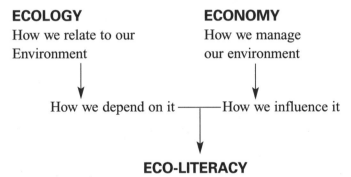

ECO-LITERACY
Knowing about the consequences of our actions (and inactions)

The world is interlinked as never before: when you ring BT, the call centre is likely to be in India. Children can e-mail each other almost anywhere. To live and work effectively, children have to learn how these networks behave and how to use them to make their voices heard. They also have to think about 'what will happen if...' and take responsibility for what they do.

This book does not preach to you or your children about what you 'should' do. It is about encouraging them – and you – to think and be creative, together. A recent survey of teenagers in Australia reported by David Hicks (2002) showed that they see the future as un-compassionate, physically violent, divided, mechanical, unsustainable and politically corrupt. At the same time, they were fond of 'technocratic dreaming' about a world where everything would be available at the touch of a lap-top keyboard.

Rather than trying to prepare children for life in such a cold, technological world, this book focuses on how you might help children participate more actively in the world as it is now. It suggests new ways in which children's learning can be focused on important ideas from their everyday lives. It takes for granted that children want to confront big issues, and that all children are able to do so, at an appropriate level. Here's an example.

> I was recently observing a student's lesson on the life cycle of a butterfly with a Y2 class. After using puppets and pictures of egg, caterpillar, chrysalis and butterfly, the student was re-capping the cycle at the end of the lesson, and asked, 'so after the butterfly stage, what happens next?' , expecting the answer, 'It lays eggs, and the cycle begins again'. Instead, 'It dies' said one girl.

How then do we help children deal with death? When taking the same children to a farm, letting them feed lambs, how do we deal with the fact that the lambs are headed for the abattoir and Tesco freezers?

The book suggests ways to deal with the really big issues such as: how did the universe begin? How did life begin? Why are we harming our environment? Who is responsible? How can we make less waste? How can we apply the big ideas in our homes? It offers practical examples that have worked for other teachers. And because things change quickly, it puts you in touch with sources of up-to-date information.

The book also questions a few myths about school learning: for example, that the best way for children to learn is through separate subjects. It shows teachers how important the connections between subjects are, if genuine concerns about the world are to be dealt with. One such example is the issue of clean water supply, which is about science, health, population growth, industry, culture, economics, politics. Two-thirds of the world's fresh water is in Antarctica: the icecap is melting rapidly. Whose responsibility is this?

The book also considers how children learn about their environment out of school: the findings may encourage you to make visits and to get the most out of them. At one level, this means children's own immediate environment; it also means using the wide range of interactive centres, farms, zoos, gardens, wind-farms, lakes, landfill sites and all the other possibilities that have recently sprung up with a deliberately educational function. It is one thing to teach children to read; quite another to teach them to *want* to read. Literacy that is unused is pointless: knowing how to reduce waste without doing something about it is equally pointless. We have to help children to *want* to learn more about their world, and to use their learning to bring about change for the better.

Young people need to be able to make informed choices, but this does not mean that they should all know everything. What matters is that as groups, classes or communities, they develop the knowledge and skills relevant to the problems at hand, so that they know where to get information when they need it, and they know how to persuade people to help them get things done.

Rather than eco-literacy fitting in with the National Curriculum, the book shows how the National Curriculum should fit eco-literacy, as a new core area alongside the basics and the creative subjects. Innovation, flexibility and creativity are again the buzz-words; like everything else, the curriculum goes through cycles of change from highly prescriptive to general, and I predict that we are at the beginning of a swing away from the prescriptive. Teachers, I hope, are going to have much more say about what and how they teach and this book aims to support them.

Tests, targets, standards or inspections are not a focus here. There are more important things in children's primary education, such as maintaining their enthusiasm, curiosity and desire to know more about their world. It is about fire-lighting, not simply pot-filling; about children wanting to learn about life, whilst taking full account of the importance of basic skills and knowledge. Sir Alec Clegg, a great primary educator of the 1950s-70s, was fond of quoting this verse from a Victorian sampler:

> If thou of fortune be bereft
> And of this earthly store have left
> Two loaves, sell one, and with the dole
> Buy hyacinths to feed the soul.

Eco-literacy means understanding the way things are organised to sustain the web of life. And this book is about firing you and your pupils to want to learn about it together and to do something about it, in your classrooms and out. To nurture hyacinths, as well as eating bread.

Easter Island: a parable for the world
The story of Easter Island is a good starting point, as it raises many of the questions about ecology and survival we face today. It is also an easy story for children to understand and discuss.

Easter Island, known to its inhabitants as Rapa Nui, is the most isolated island on the planet, situated about 1,000 miles from South America to the east and Polynesia to the west, in the middle of the Pacific Ocean. It was first settled by Polynesians who arrived there in the 6th century by canoe. They found an island rich in palm trees, birds and fish, and settled there. Their population grew gradually for about 1,000 years until suddenly they almost entirely disappeared. Archaeological evidence shows that in the 16th century, many died of starvation;

the island was denuded of palms; and most skeletons indicated a violent death. What happened? This was not due to an earthquake or hurricane: the disaster was brought on by the islanders themselves.

Easter Island is famous for its many huge carved stone heads, some over 10m tall and weighing hundreds of tons, and these were the cause of the decline. The inhabitants carved them as tributes to their ancestors; the stone heads watched over them and protected them. However, moving them into place was a huge task and required many rollers, which were made by cutting down the palm trees. Gradually, the palm trees were entirely decimated to transport more and more statues and could not regenerate fast enough. The growing population depended on birds and their eggs for food but fewer and fewer birds survived and nested on the island. Without trees the islanders could not make canoes, so their fishing was limited. Food became scarce, people starved and civil war broke out between factions over the little food left. Many people were slaughtered. But without canoes, they could not escape to find other land; they were cut off by a thousand miles of sea. The population was reduced to a tiny number, who ultimately learned their lesson and established systems for sharing the few remaining birds and their eggs, and growing a few crops to eat.

Then in the 11th century, Dutch explorers arrived. They found a small, settled, peaceful population beginning to recover. However, the Dutch brought with them the worst gift of all: venereal diseases, especially syphilis, which finally put paid to the remaining population, who had had no contact with European diseases and succumbed instantly. Only the giant stones remain to remind us of this amazing culture. Your pupils can find out much more about the story of Rapa Nui by searching the web for 'Easter Island'. A good site to begin with is the BBC's Horizon programme, on www.bbc.co.uk/ science/horizon/2003/easter island.shtml

Why a parable for the world? The Easter Islanders became obsessed with the pursuit of their religion, in this case ancestor worship, and consequently plundered their natural resources unsustainably. This parallels the way oil reserves are currently at the centre of wars about religious differences in the Middle East and Africa. Just as we are trapped on a planet with finite resources, the Islanders were trapped on an island with finite resources. They left it too late to see the danger signs, and were unprepared for an eventuality that they could not have predicted (in their case, the arrival of Europeans with new diseases), just as we are ignoring the danger signs of deforestation, over-fishing and global warming, and are frequently attacked by new diseases such as AIDS, Ebola, West Nile Fever, Bird Flu and SARS. We are doing, on a global scale, exactly what the Easter Islanders did 500 years ago. How can we avoid making the same mistake?

2
Why is eco-literacy important?

There have to be powerful reasons for arguing for a new curriculum subject or a new way of organising the primary school curriculum. Yet teaching the conventional subjects is less and less relevant to children's needs today. Nonetheless we need to justify why we should teach The Big Issues. What makes something an Issue? What makes an issue Big? Why organise the curriculum around these ideas?

In some countries, developing a National Curriculum meant going back to basic ideas about what education is for. In the UK in the 1980s, it simply meant going back to the conventional breakdown of the curriculum into the safe subjects that had always been tested in secondary schools. To the government of the day, it also meant getting away from 'progressive', trendy ideas about topic-based and child-centred education, introduced in the 1960s. As Robin Alexander (2000) has pointed out, though, English primary education periodically reverts to 19th century notions of 'elementary' education, and we went into such a cycle in the late 1980s. As we slowly come out of it now, we can think laterally about what children need to learn.

In the 2001 *Guardian* competition to describe 'The School I'd Like', the idea of 'Relevance' figured strongly in the minds of children (Burke and Grosvenor, 2003). What they wanted above all were schools that were relevant to the things at the forefront of their minds. As a teacher and trainer of science teachers for many years, I noted that science, as a subject, was not high on the list of relevant things. Nor was whole-class teaching! So perhaps this is a good time to consider incorporating the science children learn into something bigger, thus allowing its relevance to emerge more clearly.

Fritjof Capra is one of the world's great thinkers on the links between science and other aspects of life and he is clear about what this 'something bigger' should be:

> In the coming decades the survival of humanity will depend on our ecological literacy – our ability to understand the basic principles of ecology and to live accordingly. Thus, ecological literacy, or 'eco-literacy', must become a critical skill for politicians, business leaders and professionals in all spheres, and should be the most important part of education at all levels – from primary and secondary schools to colleges, universities and the continuing education and training of professionals. (Capra 2002: 201)

Capra proposes that eco-literacy is fundamental to learning and survival in the future; yet no obvious place has as yet been found for it in the curriculum of British primary schools. It could, however, become a genuine core element of the curriculum. Not perhaps another subject, just as it isn't a good idea for citizenship to be seen as a subject. My case is that eco-literacy can draw together the important dimensions of science, humanities and citizenship that are essential for children to understand what we have to do to ensure our continued survival on the planet.

This would seem logical to most teachers in Europe, the Far East and elsewhere. In most places, the primary curriculum has never been divided up into subjects such as science, especially in the earlier years of schooling. (Even reading does not appear on the curriculum in most European countries before the age of 7). What many countries do is help children first to gain experience of the world around them, gradually focusing on Local Studies or Environmental Studies in the later years of primary school.

Eco-literacy for primary school children might therefore start (as the curriculum for the Foundation Years does now) by developing children's awareness of phenomena in the world around them: materials, living things, weather, forces, energy. Small ideas lead to questions about big ideas, so children could then naturally move on to an understanding of the main principles that ecosystems have evolved to sustain the web of life – principles such as:

- Networks (such as food webs)
- Cycles in nature (water, carbon, nitrogen)
- The transformation of solar energy (by photosynthesis, solar cells, wind power)
- Biodiversity
- Balance.

This sounds like science, and much of it is. But children don't separate these ideas from other important things such as shopping, eating, clothes, music, TV, mobile phones, pets, sport. And in all these cases, there are decisions for them to make, which affect them and their environment. What foods are unhealthy or might cause allergies? Where does this apple or this T-shirt come from? Is using a mobile phone dangerous? How do we prevent dolphins getting killed in fishing

8

nets? Should animals be used for laboratory experiments? In other words, children often want to know if they are doing the 'right' thing.

Children are also deeply concerned about the causes and unfairness of conflict, poverty, hunger, disease and who decides, i.e. politics. Many were violently opposed to the war in Iraq, and came out to protest against it. Studying wars, trade, logging, mining, whaling, chocolate manufacture, oil refining and many other industrial processes takes account of children's fascination with studying other cultures. It also means that children see the way history, geography, religion and economics influence decisions. Issues such as these are issues because they provoke powerfully different views, things to argue about. They are big issues because they affect everybody on the planet, even though we often don't realise it. To take one small example:

> Coffee is the most traded crop in the world, after oil. It goes through 16 stages between coffee bush and cup. At each stage someone makes a profit. The price of a kilo of Instant Coffee is about 70 times the price a grower gets for his beans. Is this fair? Who do you think is making most of the profit?

When children become hooked on this kind of learning about things that matter (even though they probably don't drink much coffee!), they can do what they already love to do, that is re-design their living environment. In Iceland, for example, 'Innovation Education' is already a core subject – *the* core subject – and focuses children's attention on inventing practical solutions to real problems they have identified. Eco-literacy therefore leads to thinking about 'Eco-design', which means re-thinking systems for such things as food production and distri- bution, energy generation, house design, transportation, that are sustainable, satisfying children's current needs in ways that will not jeopardise the chances of future generations. These are the topics covered in part 2, indicating practical ways to promote children's enquiry and invention. Calculating the 'food miles' travelled by imported fruits, for instance, can lead pupils to investigate ways to minimise consumption of fossil fuels in transporting food. It could also en- courage them to start growing their own crops: in schools in Amsterdam, for instance, each child is entitled to a 'School Garden', a personal strip of com- munity allotment on which they learn to plant and grow crops for themselves.

An eco-literacy curriculum would require a local dimension. Sensible, 'sus- tainable' food production or water conservation would need to focus on some- thing different in East Anglia, Cornwall or the Lake District than in Mali or Zimbabwe. Children can debate problems like the following:

In a rural area of an African country, a British charity built a water pipeline to a village that had never had running water, and set up a tap in the centre of the village. Within days, however, the pipeline had been smashed in several places. Why? The nearest fresh water was a river, about 30 minutes walk away: local boys had a donkey cart fitted with a large oil-drum, in which they collected water and sold it to villagers. The pipeline had destroyed their source of income, so they smashed it. What should be done?

This is a very different problem from that in Cornwall, where people object to paying the highest water and sewage taxes in the country, to provide holiday-makers from elsewhere with clean beaches. What do you do about that?

Waste is another local problem. Re-cycling and waste management mean one thing to children in an agricultural area, something else in a city. Sixty years ago, the contents of a dustbin would have been 60% ash from coal fires. Now, a bin is more likely to contain 60% plastic. Before children consider what to do about it they need first to find out what the situation is in their area. Can they recycle plastic? If not, why not? Why do they have recycling bins in the nearby town, but not in our village? These simple 'facts' are suddenly seen to be connected to other issues, such as the cost of collection and the demand for plastic. (You can make expensive fleeces from plastic milk bottles!)

Unemployment, public transport, renewable energy and affordable housing are similarly all bigger issues for some families and their communities than for others. But within five years, European law will require the recycling of all elec-trical goods, a decision that affects us all. An eco-literacy curriculum must pre-scribe these big ideas worth dealing with, while leaving detail and choices to teachers and local experts.

This does not mean that eco-literacy must be serious, problem-ridden and joyless. Children can act in many ways: a 'you can...!' philosophy is the corner-stone of good eco-literacy. Many schools now have composting bins and worm bins, and children just love exploring these, even if only by smell. Primary schools can and do apply ecological principles: an eco-schools movement already exists and thrives (see the Going for Green website, goingforgreen. org.uk). But schools could do much more if freed to do so and if they made links with each other. Networks are important.

Focusing on eco-literacy will make partnerships more necessary and more pos-sible. Every school is close to something like a landfill site, re-cycling centre, abattoir, supermarket, factory, farm, airport, harbour, nature reserve, building site, sewage works, power station or environmental centre. These are real places, where the real things that fascinate children go on. Direct involvement between schools and such real-world sources of sustainable (or non-sustainable) activity are a valuable way for children to gain first-hand insights and add relevance and depth to their understanding. Examples of effective partnerships, and how to set them up, are given in chapter 11.

Partnerships inevitably lead to children looking at their own homes and schools, seeing how these could become more eco-friendly. In 'The School I'd Like' competition, children re-designed their schools in impressive and original ways, to be more appropriate places for learning, as shown overleaf.

Teacher training will need to reflect this re-think of the curriculum. At the University of Exeter, our Primary PGCE Science specialism has evolved into an eco-literacy specialism, in which students have an additional placement working with children in non-school settings such as an environmental centre, a zoo, a landfill site, a farm or the Eden Project. We made these changes because we have identified a clear demand from trainees for such a shift: many of the Primary Science specialists we recruit have Environmental Science degrees, and want to work with children outside formal school settings as well as in schools. Some we recruit from other countries, to add valuable alternative perspectives and knowledge. Some of our home-grown students have their placement abroad, and bring back valuable new ideas.

Are English primary schools ready for this shift? Are you, the teacher, ready? I sent a version of this chapter to a headteacher recently for his views. 'The kids would love it!' is all he said, and all he needed to say. It may mean leaving the basics of literacy and numeracy as they are, for now at least, whilst focusing the rest of the curriculum around two distinctive areas: eco-literacy and creative Arts. But it will also bring us closer to practices in many European countries and else-where. Innovation Education in Iceland, for example, has been shown to release children's natural creativity and imagination (see www. education.leeds.ac.uk/ development/innovations.pdf).

In future, there is likely to be more opportunity for cross-curricular work. Anyone who visited the Schools' Art Projects at the Eden Project will have seen a powerful demonstration of how children can see and celebrate the links be-tween plants, people and the world around them by creating paintings, sculp-tures, collages and fabrics. All over the world, music, drama, story-telling and dance are key ways in which people communicate important ecological mes-sages about crops, rain, soil, forests, animals and their spiritual beliefs: the carv-ings and paintings of the First Peoples of North America and the music and dance of Africa and India demonstrate this powerfully. Closer to home, I have recently watched young Cornish children creating a dance to tell the story of what they learned after a visit to an environmental centre. They were utterly engrossed.

Overleaf: Cara's school of the future

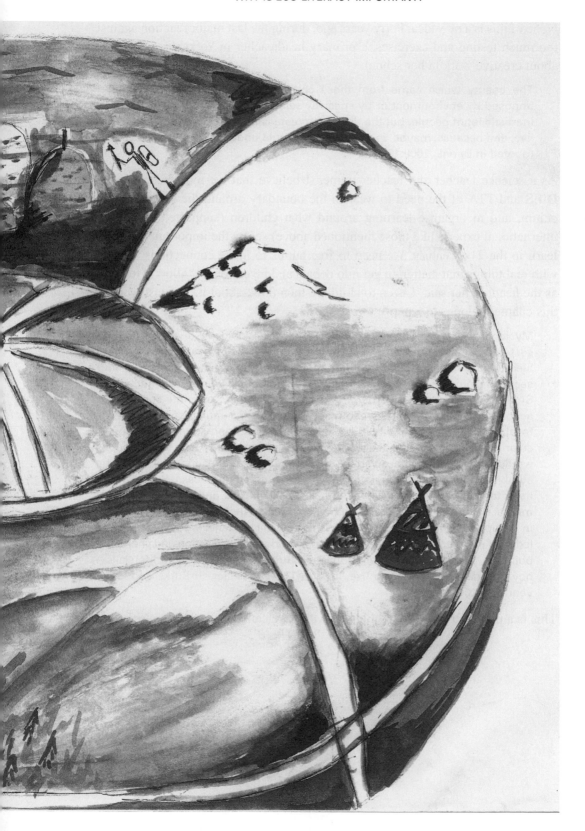

None of this is a new idea. Forty years ago, during the last major reaction against too much testing and exercises, a primary headteacher in Yorkshire wrote this about creative work in her school:

> The beauty which came from these children could not have been super-imposed by environment or by specially selected teachers, for we are just an inartistic lot of people, but the desire to create came because we allowed it to live, and because, maybe, in some way we could understand why it was there. (quoted in Darvill, 2000:13).

As a science teacher and teacher trainer, I believe that we must persuade the DfES and TTA of the need to weaken the boundary around the science curriculum, and to organise learning around what children (supported widely by international experts like those mentioned above) see as the important things to learn in the 21st century. We need to free pupils to make connections, to deal with real things that matter, to get into debate and invention, to 'allow it to live', as the headteacher said. Listen to children, then think about it. The last word in this chapter belongs to a pupil:

> My ideal school would be an entire planet. It would be divided into four sections... each composed of a specific terrain with its own culture and way of life. In each section would be a large telescope to view the terrain. The four sections would be Desert; Underwater; Mountains and Volcanoes; and Jungle. Students would travel in large groups of mixed ages to promote social inter-action and respect. In each section they would learn a variety of skills, but the focal point of the zones would be life experiences... and survival skills parti-cular to each zone. Each zone would have its assigned language so that pupils would leave school with a variety of languages. Social economics would be combined into cultural integration and overcoming differences... Pupils would have to undergo two tests: of courage, physical skills and ingenuity, and of mental skills, how to survive on natural resources. Another test would be taken in groups to test for co-operation. In this way, all students would learn know-ledge of each terrain, experience in the real world, self-realisation and character-building, teamwork skills, self-motivation and appreciation – and life skills – how to adapt knowledge to use... (Cara, 14, Winchester, in Burke and Gros-venor, 2003)

This is a powerful plea for eco-literacy which we cannot afford to ignore.

3
Key ideas in eco-literacy

The problem of 'big ideas'

There is always a danger that people will react negatively to big ideas and big words. 'Development' and 'Sustainability' are words you can't argue with, they must be a good thing – but they don't help you decide what to teach on a Monday afternoon.

So what do you need to understand to be eco-literate? What would be in the Glossary of Terms in the National Eco-Literacy Strategy Ring Binder? The National Literacy Strategy Glossary has over 100 terms 'intended for teachers', including concepts such as Calligram, Cinquain, Clerihew, Ellipsis, Eulogy, Logograph, Morpheme and Portmanteau. So you will get away lightly here with only a dozen or so! And it is fine to look at the big ideas in different ways.

Being eco-literate

... means understanding how ecosystems are organised and using these principles to live by. So the big ideas of eco-literacy are more or less the big ideas of ecosystems, or ecology: how we interact with our environment.

The first idea, that of *Networks*, is the most important. All living systems are inter-connected in complex ways and we have to understand these hidden connections to understand how things affect each other. For example, there are living networks of plants and animals; social networks of people; organisational networks to facilitate trade; and communications networks, often based on the internet and mobile phones. A change at one point in the network can have effects at many other places on the network; what you do (such as forwarding a message with a virus) has implications for unseen others. Understanding networks is so important to eco-literacy that the next chapter is given over to sorting out what networks are, and how they (net)work.

Related to networks are the various *Cycles* in nature: all children have studied the Water Cycle, but equally important to life are the Carbon Cycle and the Nitrogen Cycle, as well as what we might call the Waste Cycle. There is no waste, in one sense, within a living ecosystem; one creature's waste is another's 'food'. Cow-pats provide food for flies, manure for the fields, bio-gas for cooking in Tanzania, fuel for burning in India and house-building material in many countries. Food is composted and helps grass grow to feed the cows. Cycles are simply closed networks, where change goes round and feeds back.

Networks and cycles also imply *Balance*. Life has been sustained on this planet for millions of years through networks balancing things out; biblical ideas about plagues are paralleled now by the way over-population of species is balanced by periodic epidemics, or spells of drought and starvation. There are still plenty of fish in the sea; but if we go too far down the line of factory-fishing, we might reach a point where, as on Easter Island, the balance is sufficiently disturbed that cod or other species are wiped out beyond recovery. However, in another part of the network, fishermen depend on catching fish for their livelihood...

After balancing ecosystems in the form of Networks and Cycles comes *Renewables*: the various sources of energy that are not exhausted in the way coal and oil will be. To be eco-literate will mean understanding how energy from the sun, the ultimate renewable, is transformed into chemical energy by photosynthesis, and how plants then provide food energy to animals. There are also exciting new developments in the field of bio-plastics, or plastics that can be 'grown' and are therefore bio-degradable after use. Soon, apparently, over 90% of the parts in your car could be 'grown' and recycled when your car falls to pieces!

Renewable energy takes many other forms. We are familiar with wind farms in the UK, but are we aware that we produce far less energy from wind than most other European countries, even though we have easily the most wind? Wind energy is a good example of impact through networks, because some people don't like them, either because they make so much noise if you live nearby, or because they are unsightly in areas of outstanding beauty, or because, as the Ministry of Defence tells us, they interfere with the radar of military planes. Like mobile phone masts, they create problems whilst solving others. Impact in other parts of the network cannot be ignored. Despite this, the government has recently decided to go ahead with the development of large offshore windfarms.

Then there is Wave and Water energy, from tides and rivers, already used widely in other countries and slowly being introduced here. And bio-mass energy, which involves growing plants like willow and poplar to burn to make electricity. One such power station exists in Yorkshire, but at the time of writing is currently threatened with closure because it is not yet economic. However, many farmers in the region have signed contracts to 'grow' fuel for the power station (see *The Guardian*, May 31 2003) . What are the implications of this complex situation? Who makes the big decisions? Do they need to be eco-literate to make the right decision?

Already, however, methane gas from landfill sites is burned to generate power for the National Grid: in Somerset, for example, where one landfill site produces enough to power a small town.

Given the amount of landfill, far more use could be made of 'rubbish juice' as one child called it.

Methane generator operated by Wyvern Waste at Dimmer landfill site, Somerset.

One of the things we notice most about the English countryside is the diversity of plants, animals and landscapes. This *Bio-Diversity* is natural and exists for very good reasons. To destroy (or introduce) species that play a key part in the ecological network can have unpredictable and possibly disastrous consequences. Which doesn't mean that it is a disaster if any type of creature is entirely destroyed. There are over 80,000 kinds of beetles on the planet, but only two kinds of elephant: so wiping out two kinds of elephant would have far worse consequences than wiping out two kinds of beetle.

Some more big ideas and how we deal with them

Eco-literacy might be beginning to sound like science. Not so. There are equally big ideas that don't stem from science, and the biggest of these is *Ethics*. Children are always keen to ask, 'Is it fair to...?'. These are often big ethical questions. Should we use fuels like oil that make the planet's climate warmer? Should we grow and eat genetically modified foods, or clone animals, without knowing the full consequences? Should 'we' make AIDS drugs available more easily and cheaply in Africa? Who owns knowledge about new drugs found in the rain forest? Who should benefit?

There are even trickier questions which relate to people's culture and beliefs. Many of the current major conflicts are a consequence of conflicting beliefs. Should female circumcision be banned, and if so, how could this be enforced? How do we provide services for nomadic peoples? Who is entitled to the land disputed by Israel and Palestine? The way we as teachers deal with issues like this as they arise is at the heart of this book; it is not just our pupils who need to be eco-literate, it is ourselves, and there are major questions for which there are no simple answers. What counts for Ethics is the important sense of *Responsibility*: what we did when we had the chance, knowing what we know. What will our children need to take responsibility for, that we might have neglected?

The last of the key ideas for now, but probably the one most pertinent to our teaching, is the concept of *Eco-Design*. Because literacy means nothing unless we use it. Our observations of school groups visiting the Eden Project, for example, have shown that most children hardly ever read the signs and maps placed to help them know what they are looking at, or what things mean. The same can be observed at most centres children visit in order to learn.

So eco-literacy is no use at all unless we apply it to good effect. This is eco-design, and it applies to re-designing our homes, planning what we eat, how we dress, machines we use, and other social practices like how often we use our cars, how often we replace our mobile phone or our TV, even when we switch off lights, appliances and central heating. Have you ever travelled through the down-town area of a city at night and seen the thousands of computers left on standby in large office blocks? How much energy are they using? Could a more eco-nomical way of switching them be designed?

Another way of looking: the S-word

In addition to the big ideas of ecosystems – Networks, Cycles, Renewable (solar) Energy, Biodiversity, Balance and the human 'big ideas' of Ethics and Eco-Design – there are other possibilities. The first is Sustainability.

A simple way to talk about sustainability is 'Using without using up': looking after the planet's limited resources so that future generations are not penalised by our actions now. If we used up all the trees on the planet (and we're doing quite a good job of that) for fuel, building, furniture, paper, chopsticks and all the other things we use wood for, then life would become unsustainable; huge changes in climate, rainfall and erosion would wreck whole countries. If we caught and ate all the cod in the Atlantic, future generations might never know what fish and chips taste like!

However, this is an over-simplification. The QCA's Education for Sustainable Development (ESD) website suggests a number of definitions of Sustainability. There are as many definitions of Sustainability as there are writers about it. Most helpful is the one you create for yourself, from reading, thinking, talking, from using your own developing eco-literacy. But it is helpful, first, to consider some of these definitions, on the QCA's ESD web-site on www.nc.uk. net/usd. While you do this, ask yourself:

- what kind of professional learning for you as teacher does this web-site encourage? Is it for teachers or managers? Is it preaching to the converted, or to the newly interested, or is it one-size-fits-all? Does it encourage you to collaborate with others?

- what does it assume about ESD? Does it represent a conservative 'status quo', or a diversity of different views?

- does it make you want to know more or does it put you off?

Six levels of relationship

Staff at The Living Rainforest Centre suggest that one way to look at ESD, is as six levels of relationship:

PLANTS

ANIMALS

ECOSYSTEMS

HUMAN NEEDS

ECONOMICS

CULTURE

This way of looking might be easier for children to grasp than the abstract big ideas of ecosystems. Children could start from a question such as, '*Are the rainforests under threat?*' Or even, '*Do we need the rainforests?*'. Then we can introduce them to plants that grow in the rainforest, such as cocoa, coffee, bananas, hardwoods, nuts, vanilla. A visit to the Living Rainforest Centre or the Eden Project would be a great way to do this. Then they might progress to finding out about the animals that live there, such as gorillas, crocodiles, chameleons, monkeys, snakes, insects, and the dependence of them all on plants. Moving down the relationship chain, children can easily see how humans depend on the rainforest: a film like The Ape Hunters (BBC TV) raises important questions about the way we think of chimpanzees as cuddly pets to be preserved, when in West Africa they are seen as food for local people. Conflicts of interest such as this are straightforward for young children to understand, but hard to resolve. What might 'conservation' mean in this context?

The next step would be to consider the trade in timber, coffee, cocoa, animals... and our cultural attitudes to 'jungle' – which is how many children in the UK think of a rainforest. Talking to children at the Eden Project, we found that most believe that nobody would live in a rainforest by choice. They often think that the Malaysian hut there belongs to people who are lost, or whose plane has

crashed! I have called this the 'Attenborough Effect', since David Atten-borough's amazing wildlife films rarely acknowledge the presence of humans in the environments he observes. Children at Eden seldom noticed the Malaysian hut's kitchen garden with its abundance of fruits and vegetables. They reckoned that the people living there got their food from foraging in the 'jungle' or bought it from the shop.

Building up from simple ideas, we need to help children's understanding of inter-dependency become more sophisticated. At each stage, children's eco-literacy is further developed. One aspect that becomes gradually more important is that of bias: do Green organisations present their case fairly? Do government departments conceal evidence or distort figures to make their case stronger? Which scientist's evidence is reliable? The crisis over Weapons of Mass Destruction in Iraq exemplifies the difficulty of knowing whom to believe. Arguments about bias have arisen in relation to BSE/CJD, the Foot and Mouth epidemic, GM foods, cloning, E-coli, the cleanliness of sea water and beaches, asthma and allergies, among many issues.

Some writers argue that ESD has to give children the knowledge to make in-formed decisions about their position on these issues. I think that is an un-reasonable demand, partly because no one can ever know enough, and partly because children also need to know where and how their view can be made to count. Shouting at the TV may make you feel better, but it doesn't change any-thing.

Michael Roth (2003) argues rather that children ought to learn to engage in dis-cussion in their school or local community on the issues which have real signi-ficance in their communities. They have to learn where to find out things, how to influence people, how to act together to get things done. In other words, science and active citizenship are equal factors in effective eco-literacy, and should not be taught as if they were separate subjects.

We move now to practical ways to turn such ideas into reality in schools and elsewhere.

4

Living networks

Feeling interconnected

Take a ball of string and sit your class in a circle. Hold one end of the string and throw the ball to a child. Ask the child to hold the string and throw the ball to another child, and so on, until every child is part of a 'spider's web' of string.

When any child pulls on the string, many others can feel the pull; they are all interconnected, in ways that are not immediately obvious. If you were to cut the string, the network would collapse.

Life is a complex series of such networks. We are all part of many of them, and this chapter considers some of them.

Changing ideas and Deep Ecology

We have seen how ideas to do with ecology are changing, as we understand more about the relationships and networks that link all aspects of life. As individuals and as societies, we are dependent upon the cycles of nature and the social networks we create. This new way of seeing our place in the entire 'web of life' has been called Deep Ecology. As Capra (2002) has pointed out, this new way of viewing our inter-connectedness is not really new at all, as it underlies many spiritual traditions including Native American and African traditions, Buddhism and Christian mysticism.

Networks we are familiar with: (1) Food Webs

The first of the networks, with which we are fairly familiar, is the Food Web. Here's a typical example from a school science book, about the inter-dependence of things living in and around a pond.

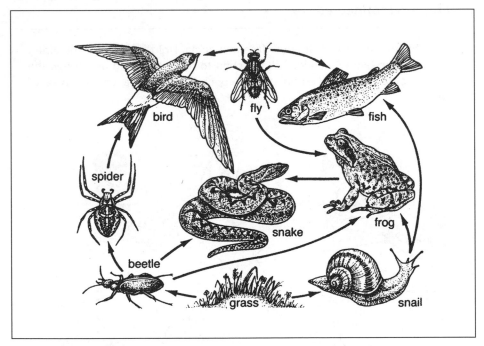

from Science Skills, p. 20

The arrows in this diagram mean '*is eaten by...*'. This web or network tells us that green plants are eaten by beetles and snails, which are then eaten by frogs, snakes and spiders and so on, until we reach the big fish in the pond that are not eaten by anything except humans (unless a stray fish eagle or bear were to come along, which is pretty unlikely). However, the big fish are dependent on many things in the ecosystem of the pond; for example, hot weather means more plants and so more food for all the herbivores, while cold weather means the opposite. More chalk in the water means more snails (because they need chalk to make their shells), so more snails means more and bigger fish. Less chalk... you can work out the impact of these changes, and so can children. So we can ask children questions such as, '*What would happen if all the frogs were eaten by herons?*'

In this kind of network, the links between different parts of the web are *feeding relationships*. Balance is maintained by changes in the populations of fish, frogs, flies etc, as other things change. The balance would be disturbed if we intervened by, for example, catching and eating all the fish (which would make the frogs and snails happy) or polluting the water with too much fertiliser from nearby fields. So the ecosystem of the pond is balanced and sustainable, though it will keep changing if we don't intervene in catastrophic ways. The links in the food web can also be seen as *energy relationships*; when one thing 'eats' another, energy is transferred from the eaten to the eater. When you eat food, you gain energy that you can put to use. Without eating, you would grow weak and simply run out of energy.

The pond is a network which has a clear boundary (the bank of the pond, the air above it, the earth underneath it) across which things can flow. So the *system* of the pond can be influenced by processes from outside, as shown in this diagram of any *ecosystem*:

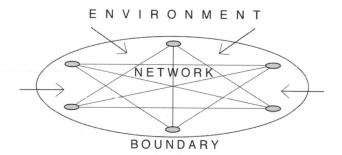

ENVIRONMENT

NETWORK

BOUNDARY

(2) The WWW

Another network we are familiar with is the internet, or world wide web. This is a huge network connecting hundreds of millions of individual people and organisations electronically. Here, what flows between the parts of the web is not food but information. But in other ways, the networks are similar, as a disturbance in one part of the net can have effects far away. Children can download information from libraries and websites all over the world: companies can market their products much more widely; almost anything can be bought electronically, including music. And posting pornographic pictures, for example, has necessitated building in filters to prevent children accessing them, and has led also to a rise in crime and paedophile rings. We also know what happens if one part of the web acquires a virus (an interesting analogy from the networks of living organisms) which can spread rapidly and close down whole companies. A few years ago, a farmer in Cornwall dug through a cable while draining a field, and disabled the entire trans-Atlantic communications system, costing companies billions of pounds!

Some of the world's biggest companies are exclusively involved in electronic networks, such as Microsoft and Cisco Systems, and have enormous power as a consequence. Cisco currently advertise themselves with the slogan, *THE POWER OF THE NETWORK*:

> It exists in your walls, in your buildings, in the air. It has the power to facilitate communications, person to person, voice to voice, face to face...
>
> To protect itself intuitively. To liberate information. To reduce costs and increase returns. It is your network. It has all this power. (Cisco Systems, 2003).

We use the network almost without thinking now, but it is also beginning to have a powerful influence on the way we live, making things like chequebooks, telephone directories, timetables and atlases almost obsolete. Will books eventually become obsolete too?

And just as the ecosystem of a pond can be influenced by things outside its boundaries, such as the sun and weather, so the internet depends ultimately on electricity, microwave and radio links and the power of the computers we use. Can it be overloaded and unbalanced? Can it be hijacked? Is it sustainable, regardless of how it is used? Probably not: there may be processes which could destabilise it totally, which is why it might be a bad idea to become entirely dependent on it.

(3) Cells and the brain

Food webs are linked by feeding relationships, the internet is linked by electronic pulses, and cells are linked by chemical processes. Every cell in our body is a network in which chemical processes involving DNA and other substances interact to make us individually unique, make us grow, help us reproduce. The brain and the nervous system, another massive network, are linked by billions of axons and dendrites, the neural network that passes messages between the brain and our sense organs and muscles.

Fascinating recent research on how we see, for instance, has shown that different parts of the brain are involved in different aspects of seeing: some deal with shape, some with movement, others with colour and others with face recognition. Have you ever noticed how difficult it is to recognise even a familiar face when it is upside down? This is because your brain is wired to recognise faces only the right way up. Because of this, some people with damage in one part of their brain can see – that is perceive – perfectly, but cannot recognise even their own family; whilst others cannot see movement at all, only a sequence of static pictures. If too much information reaches the brain, it shuts down. This is why we might have no memory of a road accident in which we were involved, for example, even though we were unconscious for only a few seconds.

Networks are interlinked

We can see that there are many kinds of networks which are linked in different ways and which interact with each other. The function of eating, say, involves the brain, food webs and the cells in our body, all the networks described above – and all can be disturbed if we eat something toxic. For example, I have a strong allergic reaction to some shellfish: if I eat mussels or oysters, I turn purple, I have difficulty breathing, my temperature rises, I sweat uncontrollably, vomit and eventually collapse. Using my brain, I have learned that I need to avoid them, and if I eat them by accident, I have learned to carry an Epi-pen to inject myself with adrenaline to prevent anaphalactic shock and perhaps death. And I tell other people about my condition, so I don't get given shellfish. I ask in restaurants if there is shellfish in the sauce. All my networks are engaged in this process of dealing with a disturbance to the system, to bring it back into balance. And it works!

Human communities

What then are the connections that make up human networks? The example above shows that the key connector is language: conversation, communication. We tell someone something and it can influence the way people behave. I tell the waiter, he tells the chef, and I get fish without sauce. I read a text message on my mobile phone and know where to meet my friend.

Networks of human relationship may be governed by many things, for example economic (money) relationships. Whether or not you do something may depend on how much you will be paid, or who is asking or telling you to do it. Power is defined by the hierarchies in such relationships: who has 'clout', who gets ignored? If you shout, who listens? Some networks such as families or gangs have developed to help reduce uncertainty about relationships. If we change the nature of the relationship in the network (for example, by putting the 'children in charge', as in the recent TV series) there is conflict and unease.

Human communities, like other ecosystems, can have clear boundaries. Within a community such as a school, for instance, there may be shared knowledge and values, sometimes referred to as the 'culture' or 'ethos' of the school. Another school on the other side of town might look very similar but have a wholly different set of values, generated by the network of ideas within it. And a school network can be influenced from the outside, by directives from the Ministry, by Ofsted inspectors, or by strong feelings in the larger community around it.

A living community is a network of conversations, then, with feedback loops: you decide to say something, something happens as a result, and eventually someone tells you what the consequences were. Information is fed back to you via different routes. You decide to take your pupils on a trip for example: children tell their parents, and back comes a concern that it is going to cost too much, so you reconsider.

On the other hand, we all know that sometimes people take absolutely no notice of what others are saying. So what determines whether or not a conversational message makes a difference to the rest of the network? Research suggests that messages have impact if there is mutual respect; if people take time to think about what is said; if both sides are prepared to listen to each other; if neither side is judgmental; and if the message is about something that matters to those involved. A message can therefore change the balance of a community's thinking. This is what we sometimes think of as growth, change, innovation, development. Is your school such a place, a 'thinking school', or is your network impervious to ideas? Can it change itself and install a new balance, or have their been times when a proposed change looks unsustainable?

Grapevines and designed networks

Some kinds of communities emerge as a result of the endless interaction in living networks. In the Darwinian view of biology, this is the way living ecosystems have evolved over millions of years, whereas a creationist would say that the world's living systems were designed by the Creator.

Networks exist in human organisations too. Some just evolve or emerge; things get known on the 'grapevines' and they change continually. There are also designed structures – organisations. Every business, club or school has its management structure, which is a designed way of interacting. In a football club, say, if you are picked for the team, you are expected to turn up to play at a fixed time, or the whole team will be affected. Designed structures usually appear fixed, whilst emergent structures adapt. But every organisation needs both: your school most definitely has both a management structure and a grapevine. How would it function without? Would it stay in balance?

If you think it doesn't work very well as it is, you need to understand it so you can see how it can be changed. If you can see what questions need asking, could you change things by simply encouraging continual questioning of the status quo? Or by rewarding positive innovations? Or by nurturing rather than suppressing conversations? You may see ways in which the management structure can be loosened (or tightened) to make it more flexible (or more efficient). In the jargon, this is called 'systems thinking'. In relation to this book, it is about developing our eco-literacy about our own network and how it functions. You may not be able to change the management structure on your own, but you can certainly use the grapevine! And you are all inter-dependent, which should provide sufficient motivation for wanting to improve matters.

Teaching about networks: the example of food

The last 50 years has seen a new industrial revolution: the revolution in food production and consumption. The purpose of food is nourishment and this has not changed. But just about everything else has: what it contains, where it comes from, the variety available, how it is grown, packaged, transported, cooked and eaten.

When teaching children about food it is all too easy to preach or bombard them with facts. Facts and lectures seldom change behaviour, but what does have impact is how people they respect behave, especially in the case of younger children. What you do and your school does can be influential.

Food is a good example of where many networks interact: food webs, human relationships, economic forces, advertising, climate change. A drought or flood in a far-distant country can affect the price and supply of the food produced on an English farm. Much of the food we eat travels thousands of miles to reach us; the average journey made by supermarket trucks is over 100 miles. We seldom know what manufacturers put into the food they produce, or how they treat it. 'Fresh' can mean many things; some 'fresh' fish has travelled 1,000 miles to your supermarket fish counter. So we need to:

- Understand the food cycle

- Model good practices for children

- Encourage them to ask the right questions about food

- Give them the skills and opportunities to find out about the foods they eat, and to make good decisions

- Encourage them to communicate what they learn to their parents.

The Food Cycle

Living things, especially green plants, are an essential part of our food cycle, as the diagram overleaf. Their roots take in water and minerals from the soil, the juices rise up into the leaves and combine with carbon dioxide from the air to produce sugars (the plant's food) and cellulose (to make its leaves and stem). Oxygen is released into the air at the same time. The whole process, called photosynthesis, is powered by sunlight. So, contrary to what many children think, most of a plant's food comes from the air (carbon dioxide), not from the soil. When we eat food, we return the carbon dioxide and water to the air by breathing, sweating and going to the loo.

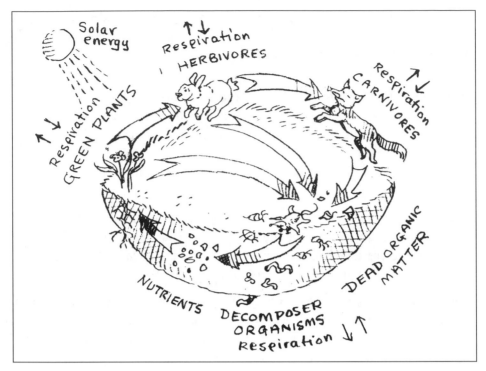

(amended from Capra, 2002 p.173)

Good practices in school

This requires knowing the main facts about food production, transportation and consumption. There are many sources of information. Some of the easiest to access are on websites or in the media, for example the *Guardian's* series on food (May 10th/16th/24th 2003) which dealt with what we eat and why we eat it. Local, national and international sources of information are available on the net. Here are three useful websites.

Local: http://www.ecoliteracy.org/pages/foodsystemsproject.html
This website describes some school-level projects undertaken by children.

National (GM foods): http://www.ex.ac.uk/itts/shortitcourses.htm
This site gathers information about which foods have been genetically modified, where they appear as ingredients, who puts them in their products, and gives lists of contacts.

International: http://www.planetark.org
This site lists daily news stories about many environmental issues, including food.

But learning about food is not the point: eco-literacy means understanding the way networks influence eating habits. Thus it is most useful for children to start by analysing what they eat and why they eat it.

What do you eat in a week?

Children can record the contents of their weekly shopping and its cost, or keep a diary of their meals and analyse these in terms of range of foods and amounts eaten. Lest you embarrass children by exposing their poor diet in front of others, make it an individual private project, ending in a report or letter to their parents. The accuracy of their evidence is less important at this stage than giving them something to work on.

When they analyse their evidence they begin to learn. They can ask themselves the following questions:

- How healthy is the food you eat?

- Who decides what you eat?

- How much is cooked at home, and how much is pre-cooked 'ready-meals'?

- Where does each kind of food come from?

These questions can be difficult to answer, and will also lead to other questions, such as:

- What does it contain? How much is 'unhealthy', i.e. fat, sugar, salt?

- Why did we buy/choose this, rather than something else? Was there a choice?

- How much were we influenced by price, or convenience?

- How do you cook fresh food? How much do I know about cooking? What's the difference between cooking fresh food and buying pre-cooked micro-wave food?

- Why do we get food from so far away? What does it 'cost' the environment, to fly foods from the other side of the world?

- What would happen if we only bought local food? How would it affect price, choice and the quality?

The answers are not always comfortable. It is the process of getting children to think and question that is important. You can help them to become better at analysing their evidence by giving them examples, such as the trade in coffee.

How much is a kilo of coffee?

Price in a supermarket ($US)	**$26.40**
Ugandan farmer growing coffee gets	$00.40
Middleman (transports to mill) gets	$00.05
Miller gets	$00.05
Transporter of beans to warehouse gets	$00.02
Exporter gets	$00.19
Freight to USA/Europe costs	$ 1.20

So how much do the coffee company and the supermarket make? What percentage of the cost goes to the producer? Who has the power to control prices? These are the kinds of questions children can easily ask and answer from the data, and the answers may surprise them. What they do with their answers is then up to you; as their eco-literacy skills develop, they will ask more questions for you to help them follow up.

What's in our food? Where does it come from? Is it healthy? Who decides what we eat?

The same approach can be taken. First, make sure you have the information you will need. Then ask pupils key questions and help by giving them tasks to collect and analyse information.

Pupils can consider the influence of advertising, say, by listing all the foods advertised on TV between say 4.30 and 9.00 one evening. Different groups can look at different channels and then collate their findings. In class, they can analyse their evidence by answering various questions:

- How many of the adverts were targeted at children?

- Which of the foods advertised do I like to eat?

- How many of the foods advertised did I eat this week?

- Who bought them?

- How much do they cost?

- Which ones are high in unhealthy contents (fat, salt, sugar, additives)?

Or pupils could count the food miles travelled by various foods in their family's weekly supermarket trolley. List where things came from, and calculate the distance travelled. Why is this a problem? How do we find out how much fuel the planes and trucks used? How does this add carbon dioxide to the greenhouse effect?

What can we do?

It is unhelpful to end on a gloomy note. We all eat badly, we are ruining our health and the environment... so what can we do? Can children resist the pressure of peers, advertising and supermarkets? How?

Evidence suggests that parents are worried about these matters, so may be on your side, and that people trust consumer groups rather than scientists and supermarkets, so a visit to or from a local consumer association could be useful. The school may already provide only healthy options, and have a policy on food. Consulting and involving parents, using the network of communications, will strengthen the impact of this. Most English children have never met a farmer, so need to see the connection between animals, plants and food. Take them to a farm, market garden, abattoir, greenhouse, processing plant, or an allotment. Encourage them to ask questions, and not be satisfied with easy answers.

Teachers should prepare themselves in advance of the visit. If the experience is quite new to the teachers as well as the children, it will be difficult to help them. Make a visit in advance; collect information from websites; have this available during the visit. Collect examples of relevant food products. Try to resist producing a work-sheet beforehand, even though you may want one for after the visit. Don't give pupils the impression during the visit that they are there only to find out the things you want them to know. They must feel they are going to find things out for themselves, to make connections, to use their minds. It is not about putting the correctly-spelled words in the right boxes; it is about looking and listening carefully, noticing things that others (including yourself) might not have noticed.

Relating back; food consumption as an example of linked networks

Eco-literacy is a skill, a tool, not a discrete body of knowledge. In studying food, children should have seen the inter-connectedness of many networks, and developed their skills of making connections. You can first ask *What happened when...?* (when there was BSE, or foot and mouth disease, for example; or when the new Superstore was built nearby). Progress to more challenging and thought-provoking questions probably starting with: *what might happen if...?*

The range of possible questions is infinite, so focus first on matters of local relevance. For example, if you live in or near a fishing community, ask what might happen if fish stocks were completely wiped out? In a city school, ask what might happen if people did not learn to cook? Or what if there were a fuel crisis and trucks and trains couldn't run? Or if it were discovered that GM foods cause cancer? Or if the price of sugar suddenly trebled? Or (if only!) all advertising of food on TV was banned? Better still, listen to the questions the pupils are asking, and follow them up in class discussions.

That's the literacy bit. But what about the 'eco' aspect? What we choose to eat determines many things; how land is used, how much fertiliser is used, where food is grown, how much water is used for irrigation. There is always a knock-on effect: for example, if a Ugandan or Colombian farmer grows coffee, he can't grow corn for his family to eat. If he buys fertiliser, he can't spend the money on his family's education. If water is used for irrigation, streams that other people depend on may dry up. Every decision reverberates through the network and impacts elsewhere.

Discussing uneasy questions

What we eat inevitably affects some plant or person far away whom we never meet and whose situation we may never understand, unless we learn to make connections. It is said that those who eat chocolate have never seen a cocoa bean grow, and those that grow cocoa beans have never eaten chocolate. West Africa produces most of the world's cocoa bean harvest, yet wages are very low. If the workers were paid the same wages as here, a bar of chocolate would cost around £5. Ask your pupils whether they would eat a bar of chocolate if it cost £5? If not, are they exploiting cheap labour?

Some Fair Trade organisations (Trade Craft, Café Direct etc) have tried to ensure more of the profit goes back to the producers. Pupils could find out which local shops and supermarkets sell their products. Do they buy them and if not, are they exploiting cheap labour? Uneasy questions, but children can face them. Every chocolate bar, every slice of pizza, every fizzy drink, is a tug on the ball of string that connects us all.

5

Cycles in nature

During the spring term, ask pupils to bring an Easter Egg to school. There will be quite a variety. Ask them to remove all the wrapping and packaging, weigh their egg and compare it with others. Sort the packaging into the kind that can be easily recycled (e.g. paper, aluminium foil) and that which can't (plastic). Give a prize to the child with the most eco-friendly egg – perhaps another egg! Let them design a better package for the least eco-friendly egg, and write to the manufacturers suggesting they change their packaging.

Being eco-literate means understanding how ecosystems work so we can use our understanding to develop ways of doing things that are viable or sustainable. For example, producing and throwing away fridges that cannot easily be recycled is not viable; we end up with fridge mountains that are unsightly and dangerous. So the price we pay for anything – a fridge, a bar of chocolate, a pint of milk, a pair of jeans – needs to reflect these added costs. If it doesn't – if we will only pay 50p for our chocolate instead of the £5 it should really cost – then the system won't work in the long run. We end up with fridge mountains, farmers who can't make a profit, or workers in factories who cannot live on their meagre wages.

The *Triple Bottom Line* means that calculating the price of something has to take account of the social and environmental costs as well as the economic cost. In a few years, fridge manufacturers will have to be responsible for recycling their fridges after use; this will add considerably to the price, so we will probably keep our fridges longer. Once pupils have got this message, they can discuss some of these issues (see box on page 42)

This chapter is about cycles, but it is also about the idea of *Waste*. If you were an astronaut looking down at the earth from space, you would see no waste on the planet; the only thing that comes in is sunlight and the only thing that goes

- Who should pay for cleaning rivers, seawater and beaches? (We tend to treat air, water and soil as if they were free, but there's a cost to keeping them fit for use).

- Should supermarkets pay the price of recycling the packaging of their products?

- Should the price of clothing include the cost of providing decent wages and working conditions for those in the developing world who manufacture them? (Where do you buy clothes? Where are they made? Who makes the profit?)

- Should we phase out petrol cars and replace them with electric cars? (Fiat are already planning to do this.) Or should we pay a higher tax for petrol, to pay for the environmental cost of car use?

out is heat. We don't dump waste in space. Our planet has evolved over billions of years in such a way that what is waste for one species is food for another. The planet automatically recycles the same atoms and molecules that make up its minerals, water and air. There is no waste.

The big problem is that nature's processes are cycles, but humans tend to think of systems as having a beginning and an end: make, buy, use, throw away. This way we fail to see the implications of dealing with the waste we produce. Even if we are keen on recycling, our thinking often stops at sorting our rubbish into the green bin and the black bin. If we don't go on to buy recycled products, we're not actually recycling anything. In the same way, industry often still sees the production process as having a beginning (raw materials) and an end (a saleable product, plus some waste). The product is packaged, we buy it, and make more waste. The contents of our bin go to a landfill site, and we seldom see the consequences.

Here's a little maths estimation for your children to think about. It is based on facts.

A landfill site covered 100 acres and took 30 years to fill. A new 100-acre site was developed next to it in 2001: this will be full in 10 years, by 2011.

How long will the next 100 acres take to fill, at this rate?

By 2021, how long will it take to fill the area of a football pitch with waste (a football pitch is less than one acre)?

The Water Cycle

The one cycle pupils are likely to know about is the water cycle, having copied it at school. A typical diagram shows how water evaporates from seas, rivers and lakes, cools to become clouds, falls as rain over high ground and runs back into rivers. They grasp the idea that the water on our planet is finite and naturally recycled.

Usually however this simple picture omits important factors, such as global warming, the important role of forests, soil, erosion and rising sea levels. The cycle is not a smooth, regular process, like the turning of a water wheel: it goes

---

Pupils can discuss these issues in *role plays*. Let them take on the roles of scientist, builder, tourist, hotelier, gondolier and let them read the article below, about rising sea levels in Venice. Their task is to suggest alternative solutions, and decide who pays the price.

ROME, January 2003 – Italy will protect Venice from the rising sea levels, but a new study said it must decide soon whether to build in other threatened areas or surrender some 4,500 square kilometres of land to permanent flooding.

Most at risk are sun-soaked southern beaches and the northeastern area round Venice, which could be submerged by the end of the century as the sea rises and parts of the country sink, the study by the state-backed research group ENEA said.

'Unfortunately, man-made phenomena have accelerated natural erosion to the point that we now have to take serious decisions to defend our coastline,' Environment Minister Altero Matteoli told reporters this week.

'This is an economic as well as an environmental problem. If we lose beaches, we lose tourist resources, and if we lose land we lose agricultural potential.'

Climate change – which many scientists say is caused by global warming – rapid coastal erosion and a fragile geological structure that means some areas are sinking, could combine to flood some 4,500 sq km (1,740 square miles) of Italian land, the ENEA report said.

Construction of a series of moveable dams to shelter the Venice lagoon – long threatened by rising waters – is due to start next month, but the project, dubbed 'Moses', is too costly to be copied in other areas at risk.

'Moses is great for Venice, but people in other areas have to accept that we can't build that kind of structure all over the place,' said Paolo Ciani, head of environmental policy in the northeastern Friuli region.

'It seems like some areas will simply disappear.'

REUTERS NEWS AGENCY

---

in sudden, unpredictable bursts. Floods and droughts are becoming more frequent and severe; ice caps and glaciers are melting; sea levels are slowly rising; ocean currents are changing; hurricanes are more frequent. Scientists argue about the causes; but the facts cannot be argued with. Humans disturb this cycle more than ever before, and just as with the ball of string, a tug in one place can have an impact elsewhere.

Cutting down rainforests in South America can affect climate and rainfall far away. Melting ice caps cause flooding in low-lying countries such as the Pacific Islands and Bangladesh. The cost of this in terms of loss of land and livelihood will be enormous. How do we pay for it? It is not sustainable to go on increasing the global temperature as we are doing now, and speeding up the water cycle.

The Carbon Cycle

In its pure form, Carbon can be found as diamonds, but that is seldom how we encounter it. Carbon is an essential element to all living things. It is the key element in our bodies, in plants, in the air (as carbon dioxide), in food and in fuels such as coal, oil, petrol and gas. Carbon is recycled in all living processes, much like the food cycle described in chapter 4. The diagram opposite illustrates how it works.

Ask pupils to express this figure in words. It is not easy, because there is no start or finish, so suggest places to start. The diagram has been numbered to help them. For example, if they start with carbon dioxide in the air:

1) Carbon dioxide in the air is taken up by green plants (photosynthesis)

2) Green plants are eaten by animals (digestion)

3) Animals breathe out carbon dioxide (respiration)

4) Trees are burned to produce carbon dioxide (combustion)

This could be called the small carbon cycle. There is also a bigger one like this:

5) Animals also make urine and faeces (excretion)

6) Animals and green plants die

7) All these products are decayed by micro-organisms in the soil, to produce carbon dioxide (decomposition)

8) Some are slowly fossilised to produce coal, oil and gas (fossilisation)

9) Fossil fuels are burned to produce carbon dioxide (combustion)

To check if they have understood, you could ask them to start with fossil fuels, or animals; and you could also ask questions such as. where does it start and finish? to check whether they have grasped the notion that a cycle has no

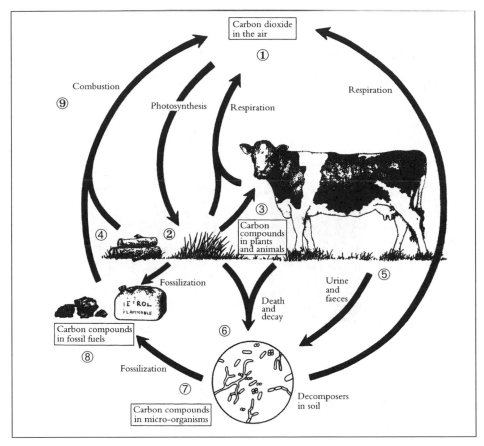

(from Gates)

beginning. So there is no waste in the carbon cycle; it is continually re-used. The process could, of course, have an end, if life on the planet were entirely destroyed. And like the water cycle, it does not necessarily operate smoothly; we are currently destabilising it by our excessive use of fossil fuels, especially petrol. You can also ask 'what if...?' questions such as, 'what if we produce more and more carbon dioxide, but we have less and less trees (green plants) to use it up?'; 'what if we have more and more cheap flights?' (a passenger jet uses thousands of times more fuel than a bus or train, for a journey of the same distance).

Waking up to Waste

All homes produce waste. Children could sort all the waste they produce in their bins in a week (keeping food waste separate, of course, and handling it safely, washing hands afterwards). They could estimate how much of it is paper, plastic, metal, food etc. They will be astonished at how much they throw away, and this should arouse their interest.

Doing the dustbins

Ask your children how the waste we produce has changed, by comparing the contents of these two dustbins.

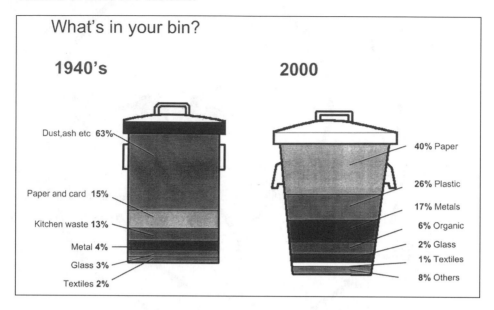

Notice the reduction in the amount of ash (from coal fires) and the huge increase in plastic (mostly packaging). Ask them questions such as:

- Why was there so much ash?

- Why did people use less packaging?

- What is the reason for all the packaging now?

- What do we throw away that we could recycle?

There is a danger that children will only think of recycling as a way of dealing with waste. Children often have a hazy idea of what recyling means; for many, it is simply putting things in the green bin. But of course there are three Rs, not one: Recycle, Re-use and Reduce. Children often confuse the first two, but they are quite different.

Ideas for re-use

Not that long ago, milk-bottles and beer bottles were collected, washed and re-used, and this is still normal in many European countries. In Africa, almost everything that can be re-used is made to serve a new purpose: car tyres are re-used in beds and for shoe soles, cans are turned into toys and decorations. Plastic bottles can be re-used as water bottles for school: Bristol Water is making them specifically for this purpose. And a whole range of science equipment can be made from empty plastic bottles: funnels, beakers, measuring cylinders, cloches, mini-greenhouses, self-watering plantpots, wormeries, smoking machines. One or two of these are explained in the diagrams below.

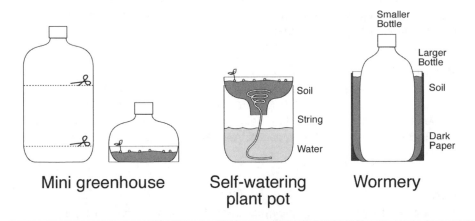

Mini greenhouse   Self-watering   Wormery
plant pot

Ask pupils to suggest other creative ways of re-using material that would otherwise be put in the waste bin: cardboard boxes, plastic containers, plastic bags, cans, bottles – for instance, paper used in the school office on one side only can be stapled together to make scrap notebooks.

The third R: Reduce

What pupils need to grasp is the connection between cycles and waste; the carbon cycle, the water cycle, the unsustainability of what we are doing on our planet, and the 3 Rs. One objective is to reduce what goes into landfill sites by making less rubbish. There are many ways to do so, but sadly, we don't. To get pupils thinking about this, ask them to brainstorm things they could do themselves. But first tell them the story of the Irish Bag Tax. When the Irish government put a 9p tax on plastic bags in supermarkets, the number of bags used fell immediately by around 90%. So less plastic is going into landfill sites. Could we, too, use less plastic bags? How? Would a similar tax make a difference? How could they find out?

Once pupils have a list of ways to reduce the amount they throw away, ask them to re-arrange them in order from easiest to hardest to do, and say why. Can they select one thing from the list that they can ask their parents to do, to reduce waste? This study can extend into an assembly or a talk by your class to younger children. The school keeper and cleaners could talk to children about the waste they clear up. Pupils could then conduct a waste audit in the school.

Auditing waste

Divide your class into four groups, so each can tackle one aspect of waste, relating to Water, Paper, Energy and Travel. Things to find out are suggested below; pupils may suggest others.

Water

If the school has a water meter, read it each week. Log how often toilets are flushed, how long taps are left running, how much water the cleaners and gardeners use, the water used in the school kitchen. The aim is to find ways in which water use could be reduced. And could rain water be collected and used?

Paper

The school office will know how much paper is bought in a year. Children can monitor how much is thrown away in a week, how much of this is blank on one side, how much is re-used. They could calculate how much paper their class uses in a week, and how this could be reduced. In particular, they could monitor how much paper is used by printers, and whether this is necessary. Paper could also be recycled to make new paper, note pads etc.

Energy

Electricity is used for lights, computers, heating, and for copying, cooking, cleaning and gardening. School bills will indicate how much electricity is used. Individual pieces of equipment are marked with their wattage, so children can calculate how much it costs to run (1kw for 1 hour = 1 Unit, about 9p). Children could monitor lights, copiers and computers to see when they are left on unnecessarily.

Travel

Pupils can do a survey of how and how far their class travels to school: by car, public transport, bicycle or on foot. They can calculate the 'vehicle miles' travelled each week to school, and the cost (1 mile = 5p approx) and suggest cheaper ways that are as safe.

They can rate their school in each category, list ways of improving, and targets for their class.setting targets for their class.

Using outside help: The Somerset Waste Action Programme (SWAP)

An excellent example of a local authority tackling education about waste is the SWAP team, based at Carymoor Environmental Centre (an eco-centre) in south Somerset. Carymoor is built on a restored landfill site next to a working landfill site, and schools can visit to see how landfill and recycling work. The six members of the SWAP team, mostly former teachers, also go out to all schools in the county to work with children and teachers to help them learn more about the 3Rs, waste management, composting etc.

Schools are invited to 'take the pledge' and commit themselves to doing a waste audit, setting up a recycling scheme, composting their organic waste, buying re-cycled stationery, visiting Carymoor, or various other options. Partnerships have been established between Carymoor and about 180 schools and the number is growing.

There are three main reasons why this scheme is so effective. First, it makes an unforgettable *impact*. Following a huge rubbish truck to the landfill site and

The Somerset Waste Action Programme (SWAP) outreach team, based at Carymoor Environmental Centre, Somerset.

watching it disgorge *your* rubbish onto a huge, foul-smelling tip is unforgettable: *we* created this. Second, it shows children the full cycle, from using to throwing away and recycling: the capped landfill produces methane which is burned to generate electricity; green waste is made into commercial organic compost; plastic, metal and glass are sorted and sent for recycling. Third, the SWAP programme is directed at young as well as older children, to help establish the right attitudes and good habits early.

To find out more about Carymoor and the SWAP programme, consult their website at www.carymoor.org.uk.

Waste Watch operates similar schemes nationally, such as the Waste Education Support Programme (WESP) and there may be a scheme in your area. Their website is www.wastewatch.org.uk

---

Construct a Carbon Waste Cycle

List the relevant concepts listed below on separate cards, for pupils to arrange in the order of carbon cycle. Alternatively, pupils sit in a circle to represent the cycle, and pass around tennis balls to represent carbon atoms going round the cycle, each child explaining what is happening as they receive a ball. If the balls cannot be passed on (e.g. if too much is being put into landfill), one pupil will end up with more balls than they can hold. The resulting crisis reflects the real crisis in landfill at present. The activity stimulates discussion about how pressure points in the cycle could be reduced.

FOOD	COMPOST	GREEN PLANTS
CO_2	DIGESTION	DECAY
COMBUSTION	ANIMALS	FOSSILS

The second 3Rs

Teaching pupils the mantra 'reduce, re-use, recycle' may ultimately affect their parents' practices. For the teacher there are three more Rs: *re-think, revise, re-educate.*

Teaching in the ways suggested here means moving away from tight timetabling of subjects and lessons. This may mean re-thinking how you plan your teaching, to give yourself more flexibility. Recent publications of the DfES support a more flexible timetable in primary schools. During a recent Ofsted inspection, for example, the inspector came with a class on a whole day's outing for environmental work and wrote a glowing report on the literacy work the pupils engaged in.

Re-thinking the way time is organised can lead to revising the curriculum-in-action in the classroom. Eco-literacy reaches into science, citizenship, history, geography, as well as using literacy and numeracy as functional tools for learning and communicating. As Capra said in *The Web of Life*:

> We need to revitalise our communities – including our educational communities – so that the principles of ecology become manifest in them as principles of education and management... (Capra, 1996: 289)

This is one way to revitalise the curriculum. We can think of the curriculum in three interlinked parts; the basics (literacy and numeracy), eco-literacy and creativity (art, music, dance, drama, poetry). And they must be interlinked. All subjects offer opportunities for creativity (see for example ASE , 2004), and all learning relies on being literate. We need also to accept, now, that all 'subjects', all learning, depends on being ecologically literate as well. Art, music and dance have been central to the expression of ecological messages, and in China, India and other eastern cultures, no clear distinction is made between the natural, scientific and creative aspects of life. In his book *The Dancing Wu Li Masters* (1979), Gary Zukav explains how the Chinese term 'Wu Li' can mean many things, including 'Patterns of Organic Energy' (i.e. Physics), or 'Enlightenment', or 'My Way', depending on how you say it. We in England are among the few peoples that continue to break down what we need to learn into artificial disciplines.

A Day in the life... eco-literacy as scaffolding

A common primary school activity has always been tracking the path of some object – a stamp, a drop of water – as it travels from place to place. Try tracking a day – or better, a year – in the life of a carbon atom, and consider what knowledge and skills this involves. You will soon note that you are engaging in many different kinds of learning that do not fit easily into any recognised subject. Nevertheless, you are learning. You could equally well try tracking your (or your children's) use of the internet during a week, and try to break it down into subjects.

And interestingly, many of these activities are cyclical – you keep coming back to the same point or question or concern, a little more knowledgeable each time. This is how we learn – building bigger intellectual structures on the ones we already have, like extending a scaffold. Scaffolding is not easily broken down into bits. Eco-literacy is a similar kind of scaffolding – you can use it to take you to different parts of the structure of knowledge about our world.

The key concept that we come back to again and again is inter-connectedness. A scaffold is entirely inter-connected: remove one bit and something gives way somewhere else. What we do has implications for others. For example, not sorting our glass into colours when we recycle it means that it goes into landfill,

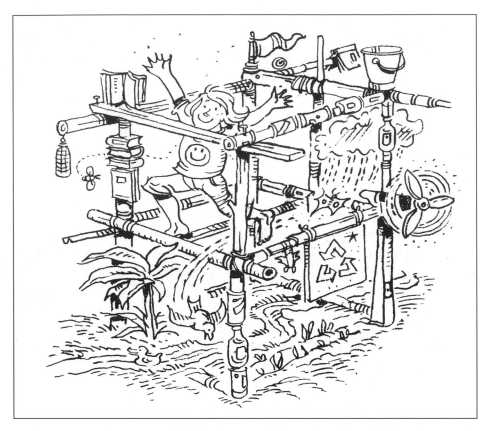

instead of being recycled to make new green (or clear) bottles. Buying all your food at the supermarket may put local shopkeepers out of business. And as Anita Roddick, founder of the Body Shop, said:

> Anyone who thinks they are too small and insignificant to make an impact has never slept with a mosquito in their bedroom.

6

Energy

Energy is not easy to understand. In one sense, it doesn't exist; in another sense, everything is ultimately an energy source. An analogy helps make this easier to understand.

Energy is like money

Money makes things happen – it is only of use when you spend it. It comes in many forms – pounds, euros, dollars, cheques, cash, in a bank account, on a card. You can turn money into other things, such as food, CDs, make-up, houses. You can work out how much money you need to buy a skateboard, a pizza or a new top. But money itself is an abstract idea. Money never gets used up; it just gets shifted from one place to another – from you, to the shop, to their bank, to pay someone's wages...

Energy is also what makes things happen. It comes in many forms – sunlight, food, petrol, electricity, wind, water. But while it is stored, it is doing nothing; it only becomes useful when you change it from one form to another. Energy from the sun is turned into heat when it reaches us. It turns carbon dioxide and water into plant food in green plants. Food turns into motion when we ride a bike. Electricity turns into sound in a mobile phone. We can measure energy's potential to do work: how much energy it takes to boil a kettle of water, or how much food energy you must eat to keep your body working for a day. Like money, energy never gets used up, but goes round in cycles; from the sun to plants, to food, to you, to your bike, then into heat and sound.

Forms of energy: are some better than others?

Energy sources can be divided into renewables that can be constantly re-plenished, such as sun, wind, water and biomass (plants grown for fuel, such as sugar cane, willow); and those which can't, mostly the fossil fuels (coal, oil, gas) and nuclear fuels. Electricity, the form of energy we use most, can be produced from any of these renewable or non-renewable sources, and this is one of the big issues being argued over at present. Which should we use?

Renewable energy sources are obviously better in most ways. The wind and the sea can never be used up in the way coal and oil can. They do not pollute the atmosphere with added carbon dioxide (sometimes called *greenhouse gas*, because it is the main cause of global warming) as burning fossil fuel does. But there may be drawbacks for some people. For example, using wind or sea can be more expensive, and people object to the noise and ugliness of wind farms. We would also need to cover half the Irish Sea with wind turbines to produce as much electricity as one nuclear power station. Conservationists object to tidal barriers because of their effect on wildlife that depends on the mudflats at low tide. Solar (photo-voltaic) panels are expensive to install, and only work where and when the sun shines.

Reducing energy used

The other argument about energy revolves around how much we use, and how often it is unnecessary. Large SUV-type off-road cars use much more fuel than regular cars and most people only use them on roads. We make unnecessary journeys, and the average size of cars is getting bigger, not smaller. We could walk or cycle more, use our cars less, especially for the school run. We leave millions of electrical devices on all night on standby, such as TVs, videos, computers, copiers. And we could reduce home heating by improving insulation. Pupils can do a home energy audit, like the school waste audit. According to the International Centre for Conservation Education, the average family in the UK produces about 20,000kg (20 tonnes) of carbon dioxide a year. It must be possible to reduce that huge amount. Pupils can check for signs like these:

- How often are heaters, lights and electrical equipment left on unnecessarily?

- Do we put more water in the kettle than we need to boil?

- Are all car journeys necessary? Could we walk?

- Are electricity and gas bills going down or up?

- Can we 'buy' electricity made from wind power?

The arguments are not simply about what is best, but also about vested interests. This is where the inter-connectedness of networks comes into play. Computer and software manufacturers want us to have more machines on all the time. Supermarkets want to offer us more choice at lower prices, in order to sell more than their rivals. Disposability (e.g. disposable cameras) is fashionable. Concrete costs much more than wood in terms of energy used to make it but we build few wooden houses. There are many examples of energy being used unnecessarily, yet people don't stop doing so.

The car

The biggest vested interests of all are the motor vehicle industry, which depends on burning petrol, and the oil industry, which produces petrol. Cars do more miles to the gallon than older models did, but not that many more, and the limits are being reached. Here are some recent statistics from Worldwatch (www.world watch.org):

> In 2000, Americans drove 128 million cars, travelling 2.3 trillion miles. They consumed 8.2 million barrels of fuel per day and emitted 302 million tons of carbon (as carbon dioxide). People outside the United States use their cars less than Americans. The average car in the United States travels 10 percent more per year than a car in the United Kingdom, about 50 percent more than one in Germany, and almost 200 percent more than a car in Japan. The global passenger car fleet reached 531 million in 2002. The United States is home to one-quarter of all cars in the world.

> www.worldwatch.org/brain/media/pdf/pubs/vs/2003_cars. pdf, pp. 56-57.

It has been estimated that California alone produces 2% of all the world's carbon dioxide emissions, largely from its cars. Whether or not these statistics and calculations are strictly accurate, it is clear that the rich countries (USA, Canada, Europe, Japan) produce most of the world's carbon dioxide pollution, while the poorer countries (Brazil, central Africa) provide most of the tropical forests which use up the carbon dioxide. But as temperatures rise around the world, trees become less able to absorb carbon dioxide, making the situation worse.

Car fumes have been shown to cause asthma, and in urban areas, it is the fitter, sporty children who suffer most, because they breathe more deeply doing exercise. So more cars means more asthma, which in turn means more medicines, more hospital doctors and nurses, and more days off school: asthma is now the commonest cause of hospitalisation of children in the UK.

How can we deal with our worldwide dependence on cars and oil? Just as seeing the rubbish being tipped into landfill makes an impact on pupils that they don't forget, so the consequences of the use of cars has to be communicated with impact. Consider this evidence.

> I litre of oil or petrol, when burned (in a car, for example) produces 2.5 kg of carbon dioxide. In a family car, a journey of 500km (e.g. London to Birmingham and back) uses around 40 litres of petrol, producing 100kg of carbon dioxide; more than the driver's own weight in greenhouse gases!

The 'bag of greenhouse gas'

Ask pupils to work out how much carbon dioxide their journey to school by car produces over one week or a term. (A family car produces 1kg approx. of carbon dioxide every 8km (5 miles)). So even if they are driven only half a mile to school and back each day, the school run is producing 1kg of carbon dioxide a week.

Take a 1kg bag of sugar and wrap it with a label that says: '1kg of CARBON DIOXIDE'. At the end of each week, let each child who travels to school by car hold it, to remind them how much carbon dioxide their journey to school has produced.

Catch 'em young to establish good habits

In mediaeval times, before writing was used to keep historical records, a young child was sometimes chosen to observe important proceedings carefully, then thrown into a river. In this way, it was said, the memory of the event would be impressed on the child and the record of the event maintained for the child's lifetime. (McGaugh, 2003)

Even though it may have no scientific basis, this story shows that people believe that early childhood experiences have a lifelong impact. The Jesuits used to say 'give me a boy until he is 7...' Recent research from Scandinavia (Hellden, 2003) shows that concrete experiences at an early age stay with people into adulthood, and are often important in shaping their ideas. Younger children are thus more likely to remember and be affected by experiences that have a strong impact, so let them experience the 'bag of carbon dioxide' when they are still young, and don't be afraid to tackle big issues with them. Encourage pupils to do a simple home energy audit with parents, and discuss things they have done at school. Help establish the idea that cutting down energy use is not just a good idea, but is crucial for the survival of the planet.

On the Planetark website, there are 20 items about SUVs (large off-road vehicles). Although some governments are refusing to use them (e.g. California) in other places they are loved and encouraged. Ask older pupils to find out about SUVs, review some of the articles, then debate what to do about them. Should SUVs be banned? Or taxed more heavily? Or only be available to farmers? Or what? Should people be allowed to drive whatever they want?

Public transport

The debate about public transport has been going on for years. Children as well as adults know about poor bus services, especially in rural areas; unreliable trains; a crumbling London Underground; the return of trams to some cities; and the increasing cost of all this. It is noticeable that other countries such as France, Spain, Holland, Germany and Sweden seem to have rail and road systems that are modern and work efficiently. So this debate is not just about technology and spending money. It is also about public vs. private interests, urban vs. rural interests, rich vs. poor interests, long-term vs. short-term planning. It is about commuting to work, about loving our cars, about politics. It is dangerous to oversimplify matters – children need to discuss these ideas. Make it clear that eco-literacy is about engaging with ideas and developing understanding, not about knowing the right answers. Here are some examples.

- In many European countries, including Scotland, more people choose to live in the city and walk to work than in England, where people prefer to live out in the suburbs and drive to work. Do pupils have views about why?

- More and more cheap flights are becoming available, mostly from London airports, which have plans for expansion. Meanwhile, regional airports are under-used. Why is this?

- Congestion charging (paying to enter central London by car) has reduced the amount of traffic in London by 18%, and increased the use of buses and the underground. What would happen if cars were kept out of London altogether? (Some European cities already do this, at weekends.) Would congestion charging be a good idea in your town or city?

Alternative forms of transport

Some non-polluting ways of travelling already exist. MagLev trains, for example, already run at some airports; they use the simple principle of two magnets repelling each other, to make the train 'float' above the rail.

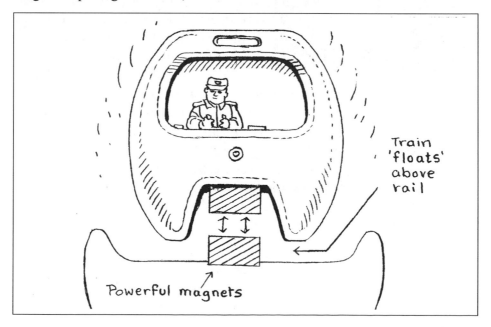

Train 'floats' above rail

Powerful magnets

The wind (and oars) have been used to power sailing boats for thousands of years, though we often forget about this form of renewable energy. Horse-drawn barges were the main way of transporting coal from mines to factories along the canals. There is still at least one regular sailing cargo ship, the *Albatross*, operating between Wells (in Norfolk) and Amsterdam, carrying soya beans. There is much that pupils can find out about. How long does the *Albatross'* journey take? How much cargo can it carry? Does it take passengers? Why are sailing boats so little used? Start with http://www.norfolkbroads. com/pdf/albatross.pdf

Renewable energy: the case for wind farms

Britain is the windiest country in Europe and has thousands of miles of coast where the wind blows most of the time. So Britain is perfectly situated to take advantage of wind power. Yet it has so far installed only about 400 megawatts of wind generating capacity and that almost all onshore. This is only a fraction of Germany's total capacity of 6,900 megawatts and far less than Spain and Denmark. Why?

One reason is that until recently, the Ministry of Defence objected to offshore wind farms on the grounds that the huge wind turbines would interfere with the radar of fighter planes. The government has recently announced plans for a huge expansion of offshore wind turbines, and aims to generate 10% of all electricity from wind power by 2010, but this has been met with scepticism. Most of the new wind farms are likely to be off the northeast coast or in the Irish Sea, but the National Grid that carries electricity is not geared up to transport electricity from these areas. So billions of pounds will be needed to 'rewire' Britain to hook up remote wind farms to the grid. Banks are reluctant to invest in risky projects. The Energy Minister said that 'There is no point in generating power unless we can ensure that it is capable of being carried to the markets which require it.' Britain's electricity grid was built to transport power from coal, gas and nuclear power stations and needs to be wholly realigned to cope with wind farms, many of which are likely to be built in remote areas with poor grid links.

Like all ecology it is never as simple as it seems! Pupils can find out about electricity from the wind on the Planetark website (www. planetark.org) which has over 120 separate news items about wind power.

Water power

Water wheels have been around for thousands of years, and they work in different ways. Here are some examples.

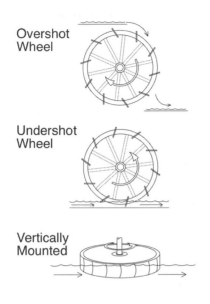

Overshot Wheel

Undershot Wheel

Vertically Mounted

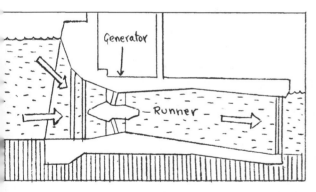

Top left:: drawings of overshot, undershot and vertically mounted waterwheels

Above, right and below: diagrams of hydro turbine, tidal barrier, wave generator (after Renewable Energy, and WMN 12.3.03).

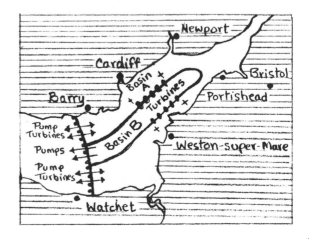

Waterwheels inspired the first hydro-electric power stations, but there are many other ways of using water to generate electricity, including using tides and waves.

In each case, water flows through a turbine or pushes air past a turbine, as in a windmill. Some asthma spinhalers work on the same principle; teachers could take an old one apart, to demonstrate it to pupils.

Tidal barriers have generated electricity in France for many years. There are plans to install huge wave energy generators off the Cornish coast over the next few years. One such generator has been operating off the Scottish island of Islay for three years. You can find out more about all these ways of generating electricity from *Renewable Energy: Power for a Sustainable Future* (Boyle, 1996).

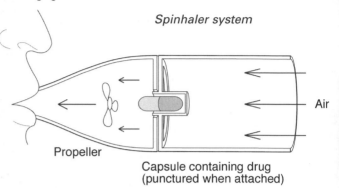

Spinhaler system

Air

Propeller

Capsule containing drug
(punctured when attached)

Working models of water power can also be seen at such Interactive Science centres as Explore@Bristol, Magna (Rotherham), Techniquest (Cardiff), the Gaia Energy Centre (Cornwall), and the centre for Alternative Technology. All such Centres are worth a visit by those studying renewable energy.

Pupils can make a simple water wheel out of small yoghurt pots, empty film cartons or other small containers. Glue them between two circles of card or plastic, and put a spindle through the centre, like this:

Water from tap

Spindle

Film canisters fixed to drum

Card disks fixed to smaller diameter drum

This can then be used under a tap, or in the centre of a stream (with spindle horizontal) or at the edge of a stream (spindle vertical). In each case the water will make it turn.

Solar energy

All energy comes ultimately from the sun. Whatever source is used, it can be traced back to the sun. Our food comes from green plants that need sunlight to grow, air currents we call wind caused by the sun heating the earth, coal and oil were originally green plants that died and became compressed over millions of years. The reason dinosaurs became extinct was probably because dust clouds blocking out the sun meant they were deprived of the source of energy.

There are simple ways to use the sun's light and heat. Put some water in a black tin and leave it in the sun and it soon becomes hot. Passing black-painted water pipes over your roof can therefore heat your water, like this:

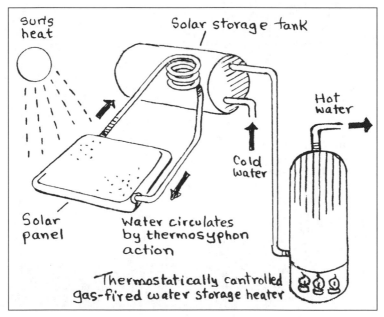

Diagram of solar heated water (from renewable energy, p. 43)

You can also make a solar cooker to barbecue food, like this:

Electricity from sunlight

It is now quite common for homes and buildings to have solar panels to generate electricity, like the one in the picture below.

The Eco-Centre at Carymoor, showing wind turbine, PV solar panels and straw-built classrooms annexe.

Solar cells use *semiconductors*, substances such as silicon, selenium and germanium. These substances exist as crystals, like salt. When sunlight hits a silicon crystal, it dislodges an electron from its place in the structure, so that another electron moves in to take its place. In this way, electrons flow across the silicon producing an electric current.

The first solar cells were produced over a century ago and used to power telephones, but they were not very efficient, converting only about 1% of sunlight into electricity. Modern photo-voltaic (PV) cells convert about 16% of the sun's energy into electricity.

Solar power is now used in many ways, to power space stations, computers, watches and calculators. Honda has even built a car that runs on sunlight!

Energy: the key points for eco-literacy

How does this relate to eco-literacy? What is the point of making electricity from wind or powering cars, planes or fridges by sunlight? There are several important issues:

- Wind, water and sunlight are endlessly renewable, and will not get used up

- Once the windmills or PV cells have been manufactured and installed, they are totally clean. No gases or waste are produced, so they do not harm the atmosphere or the oceans

- Using wind, water and sunlight means we use less fossil fuels, which are both polluting and finite in supply

- Oil has been the cause of many conflicts in the world in the past 30 years, so less dependence on oil is desirable

- We have no choice but to look for alternatives to oil, so the sooner we develop alternative technologies, the more they will be used and the cheaper they will become

- However, we cannot change suddenly, because the big oil and car companies would resist, and they are very powerful. They need time to change their practices, to make other products

- China and India will soon be as developed as Europe and North America. These two huge countries have about two-thirds of the world's population. If all Chinese and Indian families own a car, a TV, a fridge, a computer etc, all powered by fossil fuel electricity, the pollution of the atmosphere will be so serious that life could be destroyed by the resultant global warming. So other forms of power must be used in these countries' development

- We always imagine that some things will never change – cars will never use sunlight. Yet the history of the past 100 years contradicts this.

Pupils could end this study by first listing all the technological changes of the past century that depend on energy use (most homes did not have mains electricity until after the Second World War), and then predicting what they think the big technological changes of the next century will be, and how the energy problem might be solved. They could present their predictions in drawings, a class display, or a portfolio or book.

7

Diversity

Equip each group of pupils with a hoola-hoop and a white sheet. Each group places their hoop on the ground, in a different place (on grass; under a tree) and counts the number of different plants found inside it. Next they hold the sheet under a tree, bush or hedge and shake the tree and see how many creatures are collected on the sheet. They can do this activity in the school grounds but even better in a park, woodland, meadow, farm, dunes or any natural environment. Collate the evidence from all groups.

Biodiversity

The object of this exercise is to estimate the biodiversity in a particular environment or habitat. As a general rule, the longer the habitat has been established (an old hedge, a large oak tree for instance), the greater the diversity of species. The list of known living species is around 1.7 million: but many experts believe that the number of unknown species far outweighs the known, and may be between 10-100 million, with 30 million being the current best guess. And this does not take account of all those, like dinosaurs, that are now extinct. Colin Tudge (2000) has pointed out that we would not have enough words to name them all nor a library big enough to catalogue them. There are 40,000 known bacteria, for instance; but 1000 times this number may still be undiscovered.

So why worry about losing a few species? The answer can be explained in terms of the ball of string. What happens when a few things disappear from the network? Disturbances crop up in the least expected places, some of which might have catastrophic consequences. One example illustrates this.

The Rainforest as an example of biodiversity

Tropical rainforests, along with coral reefs, are the most biodiverse habitats on the planet; and it is estimated that most of the plants and animals that live there have not yet been identified. They are diverse because they contain a wide range of conditions for growth, in terms of light, temperature, humidity and soil, and because they have been undisturbed for thousands of years. Until recently.

Pupils will have seen rainforests on TV, in excellent wildlife programmes. But there is nothing like experiencing the smells, sounds and feel of the rainforest. Children can do this at such places as the Humid Tropics Biome at the Eden Project in Cornwall, the Living Rainforest in Berkshire or the tropical plant houses in big botanical gardens like Kew and Edinburgh. Visits to such places can convey to children the feeling of the heat, humidity and diversity of the habitat. First check websites, perhaps taking a virtual tour of the garden. All these are interesting:

www.rbgkew.org.uk	Kew, London
www.rbge.org.uk	Edinburgh
www.edenproject.com	Eden Project
www.bbgardens.org	Birmingham
www.anbg.gov.au/anbg	Australia
www.ville.montreal.qc.ca/jardin	Montreal, Canada
www.htbg.com	Hawaii
www.flbg.org	Florida

Preparation for a visit is essential. Teachers need to know what to expect, and how best to mediate their pupils' learning during the visit. In any botanical garden, there is so much to see that children may not know what to focus on and suffer perceptual overload. Direct pupils' attention to the things you think important. Pupils may disregard signs or misinterpret them.

Why does biodiversity matter?

Understanding this means understanding about the networks of inter-connectedness that are a part of all life. The rainforest is an example of a gene-pool that contains a wide variety of genetically different species. Many plants we use as food (e.g. potatoes, corn) have been developed from forms that have existed for millions of years in other parts of the world. If we destroy them, we destroy the genes that might be crucial to redeveloping such plants.

We also disturb the food webs and energy networks that have developed in balance over thousands of years. Destroying a habitat means removing many species of plants and animals; those that depend on them have to seek food and shelter elsewhere. Take away the food that pandas or parrots eat, and there may soon be no more pandas or parrots. Take away the pandas and their habitat may be overgrown with bamboo. We sometimes forget that life on our planet has sustained itself for hundreds of millions of years without our interference. Only in the last few minutes of our universe's existence, so to speak, have people lived on this planet. There are natural ways of sustaining life which we cannot ignore, ways which led to the evolution of humankind. This deserves our respect.

Rainforests provide people with food (coffee, nuts, bananas, cocoa beans, fish etc), timber, fuel, medicines, cosmetics, meat (monkeys, pigs), skins (crocodile, snake), pets (frogs, chameleons, snakes, birds) and, importantly, oxygen. The ecosystem is being undermined in many ways: by cutting down the trees and destroying habitats; by monoculture (growing a single crop, e.g. coffee); by poverty (people cannot afford to live there, so leave); by illegal trade in animals; by mining for gold and petroleum, or polluting rivers; and by tourism. The rainforests affect the world's climate, though in ways which are not completely clear. Cutting them down risks creating deserts, droughts and more floods. It takes a few minutes to cut down a hardwood tree, but many decades to grow one.

There are no simple solutions

Take the example of chimpanzees, highlighted by the BBC film Ape Hunters. Children regard chimps as lovely, cuddly creatures, our close relatives to be conserved at all costs. But there are rainforest communities in Cameroon and other countries of West Africa who depend on chimpanzee meat for their food. If it is illegal to eat chimpanzees, these communities will be badly affected. It will take a long time to change a whole community's eating habits.

Basic human needs

The rainforest satisfies many of our needs. Yet ironically, the main reason that tropical rainforests are being cut down is to grow food for us, such as coffee, bananas and grazing for beef cattle. Is this what we want to happen?

> Pupils can discuss a similar 'what if...?' situation that relates to them. For example, 'what if meat-eating were made illegal in Europe?' or eggs, milk, sugar – whichever might affect them. Let them think through not only the implications for diet but also how they would go about helping people to change their habits.

Insects and spiders

Children mostly dislike insects, finding them scary or annoying – in short, pests. So why not just kill them? Here are some facts about insects.

- A third of all known animals are insects
- A fifth of all known animals are beetles

To raise pupils' awareness of their dependence on the rainforests, you could ask them to list all the things they personally use that might come from rainforests, or which might have an effect on rainforests, such as growing coffee and bananas. Supply these headings: *food, clothing, houses, furniture, medicines, fuel.*

Does what they eat, wear, sit on, live in, have an impact on the rainforest?

- There are 65,000 types of weevils alone
- Insects occupy every habitat know except the open sea
- Insects have invented highly sophisticated social systems (termites, bees, ants)
- The planet contains up to 750kg of termites for every person
- Few insects are more than 3cm long and some are microscopic though stick insects can be 30cm long
- All insects have six legs. Most insects have wings, though many cannot fly.

Spiders, scorpions and ticks all belong to the same family, are easy to spot, sinister and unlikeable and hard to deal with. There are around 65,000 different species. There are giant, bird-eating spiders and dreaded, hairy tarantulas. All spiders skilfully spin silken webs, partly to trap their prey, and make poison to stun it.

Spider silk is so strong that a shirt woven from it would be bullet-proof! That's the good news: the bad news is that it is so elastic that the bullet would punch the shirt fabric right through your body, without puncturing the shirt.

Typical primitive insects that have been around for millennia are easily available for study. There are woodlice and earwigs, both with eleven segments to their bodies and with callipers instead of tails. These are easily found in damp, dark places, under stones or in rotting fruit such as apples. Pupils can observe them through a lens, or in a midi-spector; draw them; suggest what their callipers are for; study what they like to eat.

Phobias

Children are often afraid of insects and particularly spiders. However, only about 24 out of 65,000 species of spider are poisonous to humans. We probably learn from our parents to fear them, so it is important that teachers do not reinforce such fear but help children overcome it. Handling small creatures like maggots, woodlice, ladybirds, stick insects, even small spiders, is a start. It is good for children to get used to them on their skin, to learn that it doesn't do anything other than tickle slightly. Teachers can demonstrate this and allow the creature to walk to a child. Remember to get children to wash their hands after handling insects. It is better to get them used to insects early on, rather than stamp on them or spray every one they see.

So why can't we kill 'em all off?

One clue to the spider's resilience is its web. A thread so strong must have amazing applications, if it can be synthesised, but first it has to be analysed. If we destroy spiders, we have none of the original material to research with. Barnacles are similarly suitable subjects for research. They produce an amazing glue that sets hard under water and this is of great interest to shipbuilders. So take care of the barnacles on the rocks, next time you're on the beach.

Insects and spiders provide food for many other creatures, especially birds and small reptiles. No insects, no birds; no birds... the ball of string again starts to unravel.

Insects eat nectar, and bees and other insects play a vital role in pollinating many plants as they go from flower to flower looking for nectar. Without bees, crops would not be fertile or ripen, so we would not have many cereals or fruit. Insects even provide food for humans: when termites hatch into flying ants in the rainy season, they are caught and eaten live, as a delicacy, by children in Africa. The same is true of locusts and many other insect grubs. And insects play an ecological role also by eating up rotting vegetation and dead creatures. Leave a piece of old banana or meat out in the sun and watch them arrive! Ants, wasps, flies all love leftovers so are a significant factor in the network of life on the planet.

Land, air and oceans

We all depend on water, air and the soil – our natural environment – to live. So taking care of them is vital. First we must understand what threatens them, so we can help protect or conserve the environment.

We have not done a good job so far. In many parts of the world, most of the land is owned by a few rich people; the majority don't have land on which to grow food, so they are dependent on buying food from the wealthy people who own the lands that produce it. Disputes have always gone on – currently there are disputes in for example Israel, Zimbabwe, the Amazon basin. In Britain many people were thrown off common land during the Clearances and Enclosures 200 years ago, to make room for rich men's sheep. The church, the Royal family, the Ministry of Defence and a few aristocratic families still own vast areas of land; for example, the Prince of Wales owns the whole of Dartmoor. Access to this land has been disputed, though the recent Countryside Rights of Way (CROW) Act proposed that people should have the Right to Roam for legitimate leisure purposes.

This issue is well explored through a simulation/role-play exercise that considers a local example. Stepping Stones, from University of Derby Theatre in Education, is one which offers an excellent role play. 'Whose Land Is It Anyway?' puts children in the role of journalists visiting a site to report on a development being proposed. Whilst there, they meet various people in role (landowner, tenant farmer, conservationist, property developer, vicar, runner, etc) who each have a case to make for their particular vested interest in using the land. At the end of the day, the 'journalists' write a piece for the local paper, reviewing the evidence and making the case for their proposed solution.

The big issues about land are what it is used for, who benefits, who decides.

If you have a school field, or a piece of derelict brown field land nearby, pupils could brainstorm what it might be used for, then discuss the advantages, costs and drawbacks of each possible use for the local community. They could do a SWOT analysis of each proposal (Strengths, Weaknesses, Opportunities, Threats). Houses? Park? Supermarket? Swimming Pool? Skate park? Organic farm? Wildlife reserve? Golf Course? Travellers' caravan park?

In eco-literacy terms, the criteria they might apply would be:

- What habitats would be lost?

- What habitats might be created?

- Whose interests are being served – children or adults, local people or others?

- Who will be inconvenienced?

- Will it increase or decrease social and cultural diversity, i.e. enable us to do and share more things?

- Will it generate a profit and if so, for whom?

- Will it cost money, and if so, who pays?

Conservation of the coastline: Guardianship

Children often feel that they can't do much to help in matters of this magnitude, but there are ways in which schools can help pupils become active in conservation, and more eco-literate in the process. Many organisations have an interest in maintaining the coast for public access, keeping beaches clean, keeping the water fit to use, and preserving the diversity of the wildlife. The National Trust (NT) owns a large amount of our coast, and works to conserve the environment.

One of their schemes is Guardianship, in which schools link up with NT sites and properties to help look after the environment.

Teachers can find out about the National Trust's Guardianship Scheme, in which schools form partnerships with NT properties to help look after and steward an area of land. Over 100 such schemes now exist around the country, mostly involving primary schools. There is bound to be a NT site nearby. Check the NT Guardianship website on http://www.nationaltrust.org.uk/learninganddiscovery/ learning/guardianship/

One good example is at Studland Bay in Dorset, where a local First School carries out work on a piece of heath and duneland at Knoll Beach, helping to study and protect rare lizards and a variety of heather plants from becoming overgrown by birch trees.

Other schemes are run by local wildlife trusts and volunteers. One example is at Wembury Volunteer Marine Conservation Area in Devon, where people are encouraged to explore the conservation area and visitor centre, to learn about the variety of life on the foreshore and seabed, including fish, shellfish, birds, sand creatures, kelp forests, seafans and corals. As their publicity leaflet makes clear, '*Half of Devon's wildlife lives in the sea*', and much is threatened by pollution from oil and sewage, shipwrecks or by human interference. Wembury's intention is to help people discover, enjoy and protect the environment – see www.devon wildlifetrust. org. There is little that children enjoy more than rock-pooling. I have watched Year 6 boys spending an hour catching, observing and drawing shrimps, oblivious of anything going on around them. That rarely happens in a classroom!

But any intervention, destructive or constructive, raises ethical questions. Should we be doing this? These questions are difficult to deal with, but they are also questions that powerfully engage children – such as experiments with animals, cloning, growing opium poppies, using animals for food and clothing, IVF treatments and GM foods. How to tackle these in order to promote eco-literacy is the subject of the next chapter.

8

Ethical issues

It was the best of times, it was the worst of times, it was the age of wisdom, it was the age of foolishness, it was the epoch of belief, it was the epoch of incredulity, it was the season of Light, it was the season of Darkness, it was the spring of hope, it was the winter of despair, we had everything before us, we had nothing before us. (Charles Dickens: *A Tale of two Cities*)

Best, worst, right, wrong, light, dark, hope, despair... this might have been written about the dawn of the 21st century, yet Dickens wrote this about the dawn of the 19th century. Children have a strong sense of fairness, and know what they believe is right and wrong. They have hopes, fears, delight, despair. Their views may be idealistic and impractical at times but children do not always think the same way as adults and they may not agree amongst themselves. But unless we pay attention to their ideas and values, they will stop taking notice of ours.

Likelihood and risk

Many predictions are being made about the future of life on our planet. There is no way of knowing if these will come true; but those that do will have massive consequences for today's young children during their lifetimes. To help them examine some of these predictions, you can ask them to consider each one in terms of two dimensions: likelihood and risk.

Considering *likelihood* means thinking about how much evidence there is that something might happen. For example, evidence of many years of weather records tells us that it is possible but unlikely that we will have a white Christmas – the level of certainty is low. We can be more certain that we are unlikely to have a tornado strike London on Christmas day, as this has never happened. However, we cannot easily predict when the next SARS outbreak will begin, as we have so little knowledge of it. As evidence accumulates, we can be more certain of our predictions; we can infer from what we know.

Risk is a different matter. The risk to people of having a cold is much less than the risk from diseases such as measles, anthrax, AIDS or TB. An epidemic of colds is not serious; an epidemic of TB is. And TB is spreading rapidly throughout the world again.

Similarly, shooting stars are a regular feature in the night sky; we can say confidently that it's very likely that you will see some on a clear night, especially in August, when they are most common. But even though it is highly likely that shooting stars reach the earth, they present little risk to us; they are not dangerous. Asteroids are something else, however. We have no idea when one will hit the earth; it is unlikely, in our lifetimes and that's the best we can say. However, if an asteroid did hit us, most of our planet could be destroyed.

This can be illustrated as a chart with four segments:

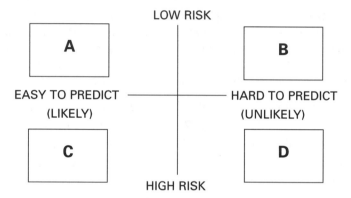

A   (Low risk, easy to predict): e.g. more people are going to use mobile phones

B   (Low risk, hard to predict) e.g. there will be very cold weather next winter

C   (High risk, hard to predict) e.g. there will be a huge earthquake in California

D   (High risk, easy to predict) e.g. more people will contract HIV/AIDS

Where do ethics and values come into this? If there is a likelihood that something will happen, and if the risk to people is high, then people feel morally obliged to do something about it. This does not necessarily mean they will: ethical considerations are usually balanced against economic and social considerations.

Pupils can brainstorm other examples that fit into each category. They can think of things like weather, health, travel, jobs, food, genetics and then discuss which concern us most. Clearly, those in category D are the ones we need to deal with urgently; those in C also imply spending more money on research and protection in future.

Here are a few examples to begin with. Which category does each of these fit into?

For younger children:

the melting of the north and south poles
putting more rubbish into landfill
catching all the fish in the oceans
faster cars, trains and planes
no rain in Africa for three years

For older children:

transplanting animal organs into humans
giving the triple (MMR) or single vaccines against measles
the cloning of a human baby
complete destruction of the Brazilian rainforest
an epidemic of Foot and Mouth disease across Europe
using up the world's oil and gas reserves
the gap between rich and poor widening further

Ethics and rubbish

Take the example of landfill. It is likely, in the next few years, that the amount of rubbish we throw away will increase. We all know this is bad; the risk to the environment is high if we do. But it is still likely to happen, because we don't like the consequences of reducing waste. It could mean, for example; not shopping at supermarkets (they have too much packaging), not using things in plastic containers (hard to recycle), only buying biodegradables, sorting our waste, composting all our food waste, re-using bottles and jars, making regular visits to the glass, paper and metal banks, only buying recycled products, using renewable sources of energy, etc. Many people find these too hard to do. Ethically, it is right, because it reduces the risk to the environment. But practically, socially, economically we find it difficult because we adults are set in our ways and also find supermarket prices lower. How often do you take bottles, cans, paper and clothing to the recycling bank?

Every decision involves balancing ethical issues against other considerations, consciously or unconsciously. Children will begin to do this from an early age, but they need to be provided with evidence and information to help them think about ethical issues. The more they take account of the different aspects of an issue, the more eco-literate they are. The teacher's role is to be well-informed

and to make information and evidence available to children. They need to feel that they have a say. 'Who decides?' is a question that needs to be asked more often. No one will act until they have convinced themselves.

It's only a game show...

People in Britain vote regularly. They vote for who leaves the Big Brother house, who stays in Fame Academy or Survivors, who wins Pop Stars, and many other TV votes. Having a vote that makes a difference, even in a game show, can give people a sense that they have influence over something. But the big political decisions are influenced more and more by giant companies, some of which are wealthier than most of the world's countries. Not just ordinary people but even politicians, have diminishing influence. If you are poor and feel powerless often the only way to take control of your own life may seem to be through crime or violence. A great deal of the conflict in the world is caused by such powerlessness. Votes mean nothing in many nations.

Your children will want to know what people are fighting about in Iraq, Zimbabwe, Congo, Palestine or wherever. The reasons are usually complex; a mix of different religious beliefs, tribal loyalties, economic inequalities, famine, lack of land, access to oil, weapons and other valuable resources. There is no point in 'voting' for Israel or Palestine, unless you know what you are voting for. So what are the ethics of these issues? Pupils require a basis on which to cast an ethical vote, so they can argue their case at their level. They need first to know and understand terminology and to use text material (books, websites etc) to gather information. Teachers can collect relevant newspaper cuttings and magazine articles, point them to good websites, then let them generate their own ideas and ask questions. Being active as pupils helps them learn to be active as citizens in the future. Children have rights, as set out in the UN Convention on the Rights of the Child and with the appropriate information they can make mature decisions.

HIV/AIDS: an example of Active Learning

This is a topic that directly affects children through no fault of their own, and for which there is no shortage of information. The DfID/ ActionAid book on active citizenship, *Who Decides?* (Price, 2001) contains a long section on how to approach the topic. Up-to-date evidence can be found and other sites searched on the UN website at www.unaids. org. It is instructive for children to use their internet Search for HIV/AIDS websites: they will find many that are reliable and some vehicles for propaganda of various kinds. This is a good example of a topic requiring them to distinguish between evidence and opinion and prejudice. They will come across organisations that provide ideas for becoming involved, others that describe success stories, such as Stepping Stones in Tanzania and Uganda (www.stratshope.org/ssinfo.html). Reading and discussing will raise questions: why are African girls more affected than boys by HIV/AIDS? Why are poor people more affected than the well off? What happens to AIDS orphans? Can AIDS be cured? Which drugs work for children? What if a child is born HIV positive?

Some facts will be hard for them to deal with: for example, in Southern Africa, many primary school teachers are HIV positive; and it is common in some tribes for older men ('uncles') to have 'first use' of sexually active girls, thus spreading the disease to mother and child before the girl has conceived. Can your children deal with these unpalatable truths? Is this information acceptable within your school's sex education policy?

What has all this got to do with eco-literacy? Here are a few questions for teachers.

*   In what way are people part of the ecosystem of a country, a continent, the planet?

*   What might the impact be if the economically active population in this country were drastically reduced?

71

- How do cultural attitudes affect the way people deal with diseases? Why are they hard to change?

- What might be the cost (in pharmaceuticals, doctors, nurses, hospitals) of dealing effectively with AIDS in poor countries? Where might this money come from?

- Who is making the big decisions about the supply of AIDS anti-retroviral drugs?

- What part has education played in alleviating the AIDS epidemic? To what extent has it succeeded in this country?

The story of St. Kilda

Like the story of Easter Island, this story raises questions for children to think about what went wrong and how it could have been prevented.

The island of St. Kilda, 50km off the Scottish coast in the Atlantic Ocean, had a permanent population for centuries until the 1950s, when the last inhabitants left. They abandoned the island because the ecosystem became unbalanced and was no longer sustainable. What were the factors that caused this?

The islanders had always depended on sheep and sea-birds, particularly gannets, for their food, oil, wool and other essentials. The sheep were kept to graze on an outer island reached only by small boat across a dangerous channel. Gannets and their eggs were harvested from the cliffs by young men who climbed down the almost vertical cliffs at great personal risk. The gannets were used for lighting and heating oil, their eggs for food, their feathers for mattresses. The first disturbance of this delicately balanced lifestyle was made by religion, followed by education.

When the church came to St. Kilda, it required the young men to stop working on Sundays, thus reducing their effectiveness by one-seventh, around 15%. When the primary school came, the best pupils (teenage boys) were sent off to the mainland for their secondary schooling and most did not want to come back. Soon there were not enough young men to harvest food from the cliffs and make the hazardous journeys with the sheep, and the community could not feed itself, so more (young) people left. The delicate balance that made the community sustainable had been destroyed. Eventually there were only about 50 people left, none of them young, who were forcibly removed to the mainland after British forces set up a radio/ radar base on the island during the second world war. For more information see Tom Steele's book, *The Life and death of St. Kilda* (Steele, 1975).

The flight from farming

St. Kilda may appear to have little relevance to 21st century children. But we are doing similar things right now. For example, farming in Britain is gradually becoming unsustainable. Fewer and fewer farmers can make a profit from milk, sheep or cattle rearing. Some farmers in the Lake District are now rearing sheep only to turn their wool into house insulation, as the price of a fleece is less than the cost of shearing the sheep.

THERMAFLEECE

Home   Product Info   Technical   Applications   FAQs   News

SHEEP'S WOOL THERMAL INSULATION

Only the big cereal growers seem to survive, and all are receiving huge subsidies. They are also cutting down hedges and using massive amounts of fertiliser.

More and more farmers are giving up and selling their land, for private homes, golf courses, pony-trekking centres, theme parks. But what happens if land is not farmed and looked after? The National Trust is gradually buying up land in order to look after it, but this represents only a tiny proportion. If farmers stop farming, what happens to the fields, fences, walls, gates, footpaths? And where will our food come from?

There are some big and important 'what if...?' questions here for children to think about. All children eat food but few have visited a farm. Farm visits are easier than ever, and all schools will have an open farm somewhere within reach. Farming and Countryside Education (FACE) is an organisation dedicated to helping people learn more about this. Their web-site is www.foodandfarming. org. Take pupils to visit a farm and then consider some important questions:

- What if all farms disappeared in this area? What might happen to the land?

- What if we grow less and less of our own food and have to buy it from other countries? How will we be affected?

- Does it matter who owns the land that used to be farms?

- What if farmland is used to build houses and new towns?

Dealing with the big issues

The big issues children can engage with to develop their eco-literacy skills and knowledge have already been raised in this book. They concern depletion of the planet's resources (energy, water, animals, plants); cloning and genetic modification; diseases; climate change; drought, flood and starvation; the growing gap between rich and poor; pollution of air and water; population growth; economic and technological growth; drugs and crime; religious belief, war and terrorism.

But it is difficult for children to explore these issues at a global level. They can better engage with events that impact on them locally and currently. Agenda 21 adopted 'Think Global, Act Local' as their mantra.

For example, at the time of writing, 150 million people in six of North America's major cities are without electricity. This seems to have been caused by overloading a system that had too little spare capacity for peak demands. Experts suggest that something similar will eventually happen in Britain. Children understand the impact of a power cut, on their heating, lighting, computers, televisions, microwave ovens. This is in a sense a local issue, which represents a global problem, that they can think about. How do pupils use electricity unnecessarily, and how can they reduce demand?

Other examples abound, and will continue to crop up unpredictably. In 2002, central Europe was crippled by floods. War in the Middle East is affecting access to oil supplies. In the mid-eighties, when whaling was being banned internationally, many primary schools did big topics on Save the Whales – and now whaling has begun again in Iceland. Is this the time to think again about depletion of whales? Dolphins are being killed and maimed in their dozens by pair trawlers fishing for sea bass off the English coast. The fishermen are going for bass because quotas for other fish have been reduced, and they are desperate to preserve their livelihood. Fish stocks, or fishermen's livelihoods? In some parts of Britain, this is a major issue for children and their families.

New drugs and medical techniques

New cures or preventions for cancer, heart disease and genetic disorders would enhance people's life chances enormously. Knowing if a baby is going to be born with a genetic disorder such as Down's Syndrome must be helpful to parents. But there are still ethical issues. For example, would it be better or worse if everyone lived to be 100 years old?

Scientific knowledge arises out of people setting priorities for what to research, what to find cures for, what to treat – it's said that 'the only science we have is the science that gets done'.

In the UK recently, the government announced that IVF treatment (in-vitro fertilisation, or having test-tube babies, as it has been called) will in future be available on the NHS, potentially costing the NHS billions of pounds. How does this get decided? Who decides that IVF is more important than, say, brain scanners, hip replacements, kidney machines, more nursing homes, more nurses, more doctors? What are your pupils' priorities? What do they see as the ethics of the situation? Who deserves priority? Who should decide?

When pupils are asked which diseases kill most people in the world, they are likely to answer cancer and heart disease. Yet the biggest killers are tropical diseases like malaria and cholera, and the diseases which are largely controlled in rich countries, such as measles, pneumonia, tuberculosis. AIDS is becoming the biggest killer of young people in Africa. Many websites provide up-to-date statistics on these diseases, starting with the World Health Organisation's site on epidemiological statistics by country: www.who.int/ emc-hiv/fact_sheets/index. html and their website on childhood diseases in Africa: www.who.int/inf-fs/en/ fact109.html. Pupils could consider why these diseases are still prevalent. Is it because there are no medicines to cure them? Is it because research focuses on rich-country diseases, not on those that affect poor people? Is it because poor people find it hard to get information and access to treatment? Is it because we don't care? How could they find out?

Pupils could also be asked to think about what seems to matter within our own system. A good example might be IVF treatment.

Finally, there is the ethical issue to do with who owns information about plants that may have valuable medicinal properties. This is a worldwide issue, one of intellectual property. Pupils can explore it through role-play. First tell them this story:

The Erucrednow tribe live in the Amazon rainforest. Until 2001 they had never had contact with people from outside the rainforest. The first people to meet them, a group of Mexican explorers, discovered that the tribe never suffered from malaria, even though there were malaria mosquitoes everywhere around the area in which they lived. The explorers were told by the Erucrednow that they chewed a plant they called Gurdwen, which had never been seen by the explorers. They collected samples and took them back to Mexico. A group of American scientists from Richplant, a big drug company, heard about this. They asked the Mexicans for samples, analysed the plant and discovered it contained a previously unknown drug. They tested it on volunteers travelling to the Amazon, and found that they did not get Malaria, even though they were bitten by mosquitoes. Richplant sent scientists to the Amazon immediately to collect more Gurdwen. They asked the Erucrednow to show them where it grew. Soon Richplant were growing, purifying and selling the wonder drug all over the world, making huge profits.

Now ask your children to take on roles; the Erucrednow Indians, the Mexican Explorers, the Richplant Scientists and Management, Pharmacists, Travellers going to malarial areas, and finally Journalists. Put questions to them such as:

• Who should benefit from this discovery?

• If the Gurdwen drug is being sold for $5 a pill, how much of this should go to whom?

• How much of this money should come to the Erucrednow?

• What has happened to the Erucrednow now that Gurdwen is being grown commercially?

• How should the Mexican explorers be rewarded?

• What might this do to the eco-system in the rainforest where the Erucrednow live?

• What do the Pharmacists want?

• What obligations do Richplant have to the tribe and to the Mexican explorers?

• Who owns the knowledge about Gurdwen?

Let your pupils have a 'big meeting', in role, in the rainforest, to settle these matters. It would be an ideal activity after a visit to the Eden Project or The Living Rainforest. Let the journalists take notes and produce Front Page stories (tabloid-style, broadsheet-style), with headlines and pictures. Let the rest then decide which stories are fair to them.

This is not an entirely hypothetical scenario, as this recent Reuter's article shows:

SCIENTISTS ANALYSE ANTI-MALARIAL CHINESE SHRUB
UK: August 21, 2003

LONDON – Scientists in Britain say they may have solved the mystery of how plant extracts taken from an aromatic Chinese shrub help combat malaria. They say that if their theory proves correct, it could lead to the production of a new generation of drugs to treat a disease which kills as many people each day as died in the Sept. 11 attacks on the World Trade Centre.

The Chinese have used the plant extracts, known as artemisinins, for hundreds if not thousands of years. Known in China as Quingao, Artemisia is mentioned in Chinese texts dating from the fourth century as a treatment for fevers. In the early 1970s, Chinese scientists developed a compound made from the extracts which helps treat malaria. Since then, artemisinins have been used widely to fight the disease. Scientist Dr. Krishna hopes the research will lead to the production of synthetic artemisinins which are even more effective than natural artemisinins.

'We've made a good start. Let's see if we can take this further,' he told Reuters. 'I'd certainly be talking to chemists about the possibility of making synthetic artemisinins.'

Artemisinins have the added bonus that they have few known side effects and – as yet – are impervious to resistance. Gideon Long, REUTERS NEWS SERVICE

Future scenarios

These are important issues for now and for the future. Young people care passionately about the future – but do we take time to listen to what they think? In his book *Lessons for the Future* (2002), Dave Hicks presents a fascinating picture of young people's hopes and fears, which often mirror each other. They tend to focus on the environment, personal safety and quality of life. His view is that teachers do not devote enough time and attention to the future – for Hicks it is the 'missing dimension' in the curriculum. One way for pupils to consider the future, he suggests, is by using scenarios.

> Try this for yourself. Draw or describe a future scenario for your town, village or community. (You will find examples to help you in Hicks pp.48-51.) You might try scenarios that are idealistic, romantic, technologically developed, sustainable, or disastrous. Ask your pupils to do likewise. Then talk about each scenario with the class. Would you like to live in it? What are the good things and the bad things about it? Who will benefit, and who will lose in such a scenario?

Some African peoples say that they have 'a memory of the future'. Ask pupils what their memory of the future might be and to write about it creatively in poems or stories, or draw, dramatise and make music about it. Pupils should express their views and feelings. This is not something to teach as right or wrong to feel, and not a topic for tests. It is a way to help them become more eco-literate.

9
Balance and partnership

Look at the pictures opposite and think about balance. How many examples of balance can you see? Bridges, boats, people on bikes ... but the most significant example is the water in the river. It flows all the time; the water changes, sometimes it is clear and sometimes cloudy, but the level remains more or less constant, though floods can raise the level, putting it temporarily out of balance. Balance is restored because the water flows away faster over the weir during a flood.

Water is being recycled constantly on the planet, by evaporation, condensation, gravity, respiration, transpiration, ocean currents, tides. There are many scientists who believe that global warming is speeding up the process, giving us more hot weather, more frequent droughts and storms, more floods. But the water is not disappearing. It is simply moving around faster.

To respond to this recent news item, pupils might need to look at a globe, to work out the full implications.

> Global warming will melt most of the Arctic icecap in summertime by the end of the century, a report showed yesterday. The three-year international study indicated that ice around the North Pole had shrunk by 7.4 percent in the past 25 years with a record small summer coverage in September 2002. 'The summer ice cover in the Arctic may be reduced by 80 percent at the end of the 21st century,' said Norwegian Professor Ola Johannessen, the main author of the report funded by the European Commission.
>
> 'The Arctic Barents Sea north of Russia and Norway could be free of ice even in winter by the end of the century', said Johannesssen. 'This will make it easier to explore for oil, it could open the Northern Sea Route between the Atlantic and Pacific oceans.' The Northern Sea passage could save shippers about 10 days on a trip from Japan to Europe. Johannessen said that the report also indicated that a recent thinning of the polar icecap was linked to human emissions of gases like carbon dioxide. The new survey added to evidence of a gradual thinning of the icecap and gave firmer signs that human

emissions, such as exhausts from cars and factories, were mainly to blame. Climate experts say that polar areas are heating up more than other regions. REUTERS NEWS SERVICE, 2003

The plusses and minuses of this can be listed. Who gains? Who loses?

A simple way for your children to observe balance at work is to germinate seeds in a mini-greenhouse made from a plastic drinks bottle, like this:

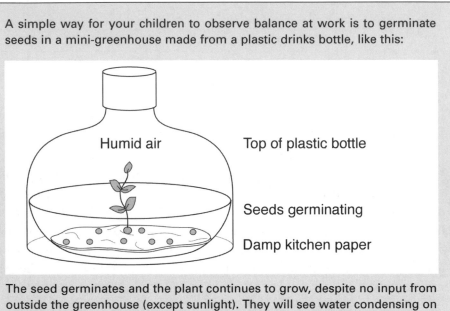

Humid air

Top of plastic bottle

Seeds germinating

Damp kitchen paper

The seed germinates and the plant continues to grow, despite no input from outside the greenhouse (except sunlight). They will see water condensing on the 'roof' of the greenhouse and running back down. The plant absorbs carbon dioxide, and produces oxygen. The system is in balance, and the plant grows.

Our planet has managed to keep itself in balance for millions of years. The cycles discussed in chapter 5 are the main ways in which balance has been maintained. But we are now interfering with this balance in dangerous ways, just as the Easter Islanders did when they cut down their palm trees.

One way of dealing with this is to take the idea that 'waste is food' and set up partnerships so that waste is not thrown away but made use of by someone else. Capra gives us an example of this on a Colombian coffee farm.

Ask your children to interpret this diagram, starting from the coffee plant itself. Worms are added to the green waste from the coffee plants to produce compost for the garden, and more worms to feed poultry. Water and compost help grow mushrooms which are used to feed pigs and cattle. The manure from these is digested to make bio-gas that is burned to provide heat energy. The products are coffee beans, garden vegetables, pigs, cattle and chickens; there is virtually no waste.

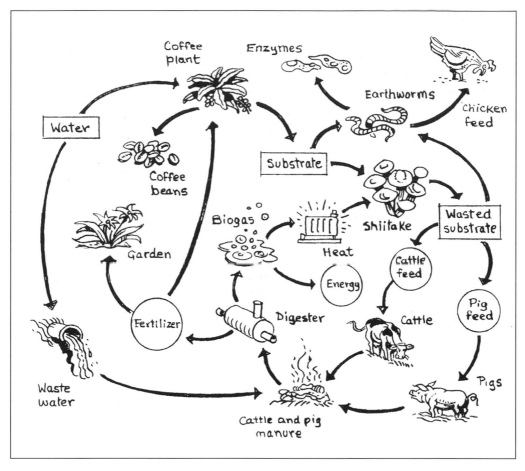

Modification of Capra diagram, p. 207

If the coffee farmer had not been in partnership with the mushroom grower and the animal farmer there would have been much more waste (the coffee beans are only 4% of the coffee bush), and these other farmers would have to buy more animal food.

This way of working is called *zero emissions* and is now being practised in many industries such as forestry, paper, brewing, palm oil production. You can find out much more about it on www.zeri.org.

Your school can probably set up partnerships to use waste rather than throw it away, beginning with paper or water. Pupils can think of ways for 'waste' paper from school to be re-used, by linking up with others who have a use for it. And they can suggest uses for the wasted water they allow to run into the drains, for example to water plants.

Some simple examples of balance

When one thing changes, other things have to adapt to restore the balance. The word balance is used in many contexts and pupils need to distinguish between them. A simple example is two children on a see-saw; if one moves and unbalances it, the other has to move to re-balance. Another example is the 'pick up the pound' test.

Ask a child to stand with her back and heels against the wall, and place a pound coin at her feet. Tell her that if she can pick up the coin without moving her feet or falling over, the coin is hers!

This is impossible because as she bends down to touch the coin, she has to push out her bottom to keep in balance, but the wall prevents her from doing so.

The surprising example is the balancing ruler. All you need is a longish, thin stick, such as a metre ruler or even a breadstick (see box opposite).

Adaptation

Once pupils have the idea of balance in different contexts, they can think about adaptation. Adaptation is what brings things into balance: how did the child on the see-saw adapt? Pupils are now ready to think of habitats or ecosystems in balance, such as a pond. If one thing changes, how do the others adapt? For example in very dry weather, the water flowing into the pool dries up, so the oxygen levels in the pond drop. How do the fish adapt? They eat less and stay still, near the surface, so that they use less energy and obtain maximum oxygen (there is more near the surface, where water is in contact with air). Goldfish are good at this; they have adapted to life in water with little oxygen. Trout could not survive, as they need plenty of oxygen. Fish have also adapted by evolving fins to help them move about quickly, to make water flow through their gills, to catch food and avoid predators.

Balance the stick on the index finger of each hand, like this:

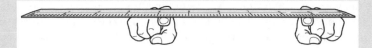

Ask the class to predict what will happen when you move your fingers together slowly until they are touching. Try it before you read on! Most children predict that it will tip over, because it is unbalanced. But it never does, no matter where you place your fingers to start with. They will say you have cheated, or that your fingers are sticky, so let them try it. It always ends up balanced, with both fingers in the centre. This is because friction is different depending on how far your fingers are from the centre, so the outer finger always moves on its own, until it they are equidistant from the centre.

Similarly, ducks have developed webbed feet, polar bears thick fur, hawks have sharp claws, chameleons change colour. Without these characteristics, they could not survive in the habitats they live in. What adaptions did humans make? The most obvious is that we learned to walk on two legs instead of four, to free our upper limbs for other uses, such as carrying and using tools, and making gestures to communicate.

Pupils can think of common plants and how they have adapted. Cactus plants have thick stems to hold water, tulips are brightly coloured to attract insects, roses have scent to attract insects and thorns to discourage grazers, nettles sting, to discourage grazers. A visit to somewhere like the Eden Project will help them work out how trees have adapted to different environments, or they can investigate this on the Eden website (www.edenproject.com).

Sharing resources: the importance of water

This book has discussed diseases, genetic modification, global warming and other issues with scientific, economic, social and ethical aspects. All will help develop children's eco-literacy. But the biggest issue of all is water. It is potentially the cause of the biggest environmental disaster on the planet, and it is a resource we all have to share. Working in partnership, balancing out the needs of different parts of the network of life, is absolutely crucial where water is concerned.

The impact of statistics

If it has impact, it will be remembered; and the statistics about water can certainly have impact on pupils, especially if you illustrate them with concrete examples, like this:

Ask pupils how much water they use in a day. They can estimate it in litres, buckets, whatever. They will be surprised to know that averaged across the UK, the daily water consumption works out at about 475 litres (50 buckets full) per person per day, or about 1,500 buckets for your class. This is two buckets per person per hour, day and night! Fill two buckets and label them MY HOURLY WATER CONSUMPTION and put them on view in your classroom.

How much water do pupils think their bodies contain? An average child has about 25 litres – two big buckets full. Over half is in the cells, the rest in the blood and tissue fluids. A child needs to drink 2-4 litres a day to sustain these levels or they become dehydrated. This is serious because without water, none of the essential body functions can take place. Their blood will thicken, they slow down and become tired, then the micro-organisms that metabolise food cease to grow, so they can't digest their food.

How do we keep our water levels in balance? We take it in by drinking, and lose it by breathing, sweating and urinating. Drinking too much water is better than drinking too little.

Ask pupils how much water they drink in a day. Is it enough? Have four 1-litre water bottles full, for them to see and feel the quantity. Now explain to them that in much of the developing world, poor people – mostly women and girls – have to walk on average 6 km a day to fetch water, carrying around 20 litres (2 buckets full) at a time. Let them try carrying the two buckets of water around the classroom, or preferably outside.

Why do we use so much water? Let the class list all the things they use water for in a day. Make sure they don't forget things they use that contain water – like soft drinks – and the water that is used for them by others, such as growing their food, washing their clothes, making newspapers and magazines, power stations, cleaning their family's car.

This can be turned into a chart like the one opposite. How much water is used for what?

Washing machine (one load)	200 litres
Bath	75
Shower	25
Flushing toilet	20
Brushing teeth	?
Dishwasher	?
Drinking	?
Cooking	?
Watering plants	?
??	
??	

The object is to get pupils to think about how we can use less water. But some will want to know why it matters, since we have plenty of water in Britain, and since it is constantly being recycled. That's a good question.

The main point to make when answering is that water costs money and people's time – to collect it, clean it, transport it, meter it, remove it and re-process it, to prevent it flooding, and much else. The more we use, the more it costs.

How much water do people use in other countries?

This graph shows how much water is used per person per year, in cubic metres (m3).

(1m^3 – 1,000 litres – as much as filling a car with petrol 20 times – about 100 buckets full).

Put these figures into pictorial form

Country	Water use per person per year (m3)
Congo	20
Tanzania	40
Botswana	83
United Kingdom	160
Ireland	326
Russia	520
Malaysia	630
Pakistan	1260
USA	1844
Iraq	2368

Some countries use a hundred times more water than others. The UK uses relatively little, but it is poor countries that use the least. Can pupils explain these huge differences: for example, most water is used on irrigation, agriculture and industry. Poor people have less technology (pipelines, boreholes, taps, reservoirs), so have to carry more and therefore use less.

Clean water and sanitation

The next statement will surprise pupils.

> *The water a person drinks in London has already been through seven stomachs.*

Water is taken from rivers and reservoirs, purified and supplied to your tap; then the waste goes back to a sewage works, into a river, and the cycle begins again. People higher up the Thames Valley, in Oxford, Henley, Reading, Maidenhead and Richmond, may already have 'used' the same water. Pupils may want to talk about this odd idea.

And here's a '*what if...?*' for them to think about:

What if people in London only had access to water direct from the River Thames, that was not purified?

Charles Dickens often described the state of the Thames in London, with dead bodies and other unmentionables floating in it. For example in *Our Mutual Friend*, one character makes his living recovering and selling corpses from the river. The Thames is a good deal cleaner now, but sadly, that is still the situation experienced by over one billion people in the world. I have watched people in India taking water for cooking from stagnant ditches and rivers where raw sewage is flowing in just metres away.

Can pupils or teachers get their heads round 1 billion? It is several times the population of Europe. What happens to these people? They suffer from water-borne diseases including diarrhoea, cholera, dysentery, typhoid, bilharzia and trachoma, the main cause of preventable blindness. Children know what diarrhoea is like – dysentery is far worse. It saps the sufferer's energy and their ability to work and grow food. If children are poorly nourished, they are more likely to catch diseases, so the cycle goes on. Typhoid alone kills almost 1 million people annually; yet in the west we hardly hear of it, because we drink clean water.

We and our pupils take for granted that the water in our taps is clean, and that there are flush toilets to prevent contaminating water supplies. School children may complain about the school toilets, as many do, according to a recent survey, but they are the lucky minority in the world. How would they manage without toilets?

Over 1 billion people don't have clean drinking water; and over 2 billion don't have toilets. The UN wants to halve these figures by 2015 – about the time today's primary pupils will be graduating, starting work, maybe starting their own home and family. The UN estimates that meeting the clean water target will cost £6 billion and that hitting the sanitation target will cost another £11 billion. A lot of money? Much less than the cost of the recent war in Iraq.

Not all countries support these important UN targets. The US is still blocking the sanitation target. And at present, only 5% of the total world aid to poor countries is spent on water and sanitation. Yet hand-pumps cost only about £450 each, and a well to provide clean water can be put in for only £1,500.

Where is all the water?

We tend to think of our water being in rivers and lakes, but only a tiny fraction of the earth's water is fresh. And we may one day have access to another huge reservoir of water – on the moon – which could contain as much as 6000 million tons of ice. But most of our fresh water is underground, with some trapped in the icecaps. Almost all the water on earth is in the oceans, and this salt water contains many dissolved chemicals such as sodium chloride, bromine and magnesium. Sea water can be purified to make it drinkable, but this is still very expensive, as it needs huge amounts of energy to evaporate the water. It is however carried out in places like the Middle East, where water is scarce and energy is cheap. The diagram shows how it is done.

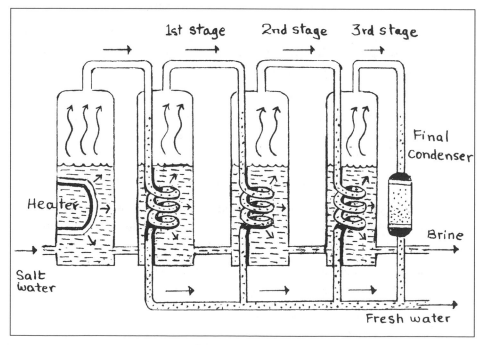

Diagram of MED distillation plant (Unilever, p. 52)

Because of its chemicals, sea water cannot be used for irrigation, as it would not only kill plants but also contaminate the groundwater, making it unfit to drink. With so little fresh water available, and increasing demand, we have to be more and more alert to ways we can save water, and how to keep it free from pollution.

Water pollution

This topic is familiar to most children. They can probably list many of the causes of pollution, such as chemical spillage, fertilisers, industrial waste, detergents etc. You may be able to take them to a water treatment plant or sewage works, to see how water is kept clean for use. Here is another statistic that might have an impact:

> **A town of around 25,000 people produces 5 million litres (half a million buckets full) of raw sewage every day.**

Someone has to deal with this. The main kinds of water pollution are:

- *Suspended solids* (e.g. from paper making, sewage, quarrying). These are the things that make water look cloudy and that have to be filtered out before water is fit to use. Other examples of suspended solids may help pupils understand the concept. Milk is a good example of a suspension.

- *Toxic substances* – oil, salt, pesticides, industrial chemicals. Toxins are substances that are dangerous to living things. They present the biggest problems, as they are often dissolved (so can't be filtered), can kill wildlife quickly and are the most difficult and costly to remove.

- *Nutrients* – plant 'foods' such as fertilisers – that encourage algae growth. Algae often grow on the surface; they are decomposed by micro-organisms that use up lots of oxygen from the water, so depriving fish and other water creatures.

- *Heating* – from power stations. Hot water dissolves less oxygen than cold water, which is why many fish prefer cold sea water. All organisms find it harder to live in warm water.

How does industry respond to pollution? There are four main ways.

- *Inaction* – in some cases, they do nothing. They let pollution occur, hoping that someone else will clean it up. Fortunately, legislation has made this less common in the UK, though not in all countries.

- *Remediation* – putting right the pollution they have caused. But this may often be too late as fish and shellfish may all have been killed.

- *Clean-up technology* – which involves treating waste water before it is returned to rivers. Chemical plants have to do this, as any pollution they might cause could be disastrous.

- *Clean technology* – where industries use processes that do not pollute in the first place. For example, using renewable energy is cleaner than using power-stations.

> Ask pupils to discuss which of these is the best. And also what is meant by the idea that 'the polluter pays' and how this might work.

You can read more about 'the polluter pays' on www.planetark.org/dailynews story.cfm?newsid=18573. It discusses cases like Spain's worst ecological disaster, the Donana incident, when a waste pond from a zinc mine burst, flooding the surrounding area with toxic chemicals and causing serious damage to wildlife in a nearby national park. Ask pupils:

> Is it fair that the public has to pay for damage caused by activities from which companies are making profits?

To keep our global ecosystem in balance, animals have for millions of years returned their waste (urine and faeces) to roughly the same place as their food came from, so that it could be absorbed by plants to produce more food. But our increasingly urbanised communities don't do this: we extract the sludge of pollutants in sewage plants, and have therefore to fertilise land artificially. Organic farming is a way of avoiding this: instead of using artificial chemicals, the waste can be re-used as fertiliser.

Water wars

When water was first privatised in the UK in the 1990s, many people objected on grounds that water cannot be owned, as it belongs to everybody. Yet water in the UK is now 'owned', largely by foreign multinational companies. So disputes about water are likely. This is already beginning to happen in some parts of the world. It is the exact opposite of partnership. It provokes *'What if...?'* scenarios. What if your country does not have an adequate supply of clean water, or if this supply is unreliable, as in Ethiopia and some other African states? What if a neighbouring country has adequate water and can supply it to you by dams, pipelines etc? What if you fall out with this neighbour, and they refuse to supply you?

Pupils can try to predict where in the world 'water wars' are most likely in future. Which countries are growing fastest? Which have least natural water supplies? Which need most water? Which countries are at war with their neighbours? Here is one example from a recent news item. You can read the rest on the Planetark web-site, at www.planetark.org/dailynewsstory.cfm? newsid= 21731.

A good simulation for pupils can be based on the example of the river Euphrates, which flows from Turkey through Syria, Iraq and Iran before entering the Arabian Gulf. Create a simple map (or see the *Guardian's* 'Water' supplement, 23rd August 2003) with brief background information. Big dams in Turkey and Syria are reducing the water supply to countries further south.

Divide the class into two groups. In each, pupils take roles such as Prime Minister, dam builders (civil engineers), chief water engineer, industrialist, farmers, soldiers, imam. Most of these are men, so make sure the girls represent the interests of women. Each group makes a case for their position. Why do we need water? What is the problem? Who is causing it? What do we want them to do? What will we do in return? How can we make sure this happens? How do we make our voice heard?

The Social Benefits of Water

Water, however, has huge social benefits from which we all benefit. We need to celebrate and protect them. Water is important for many leisure activities, such as sailing, swimming, diving, canoeing, and board sports like surfing. And these leisure activities are universal. The children in the picture below live in Botswana, one of the driest countries in Africa, and are taking a swim after school in the Okavango river, in a remote part of the country.

PALESTINIANS GET THIRSTIER UNDER ISRAELI CLAMPDOWN
August 5, 2003

AL-DHAHRIYEH – The Khabirat family postpones having a bath as they await the next water tanker to replenish their well in parched Palestinian territory under Israeli blockade.

The tanker driver has to sneak a hose through a tunnel under a highway reserved for Israeli traffic to access his well on the other side, then take long detours on atrocious back roads to reach homes like the Khabirats'.

Palestinians, especially in the arid southern West Bank, ration and improvise to offset water shortages aggravated by Israel's closure of their area, imposed after suicide bombings.

Arduous, roundabout routes inflate delivery prices for people already impoverished by the closure that, along with worsening drought, has highlighted a long unequal contest to control water that is central to Middle Eastern conflict.

Israel takes 80 percent of the West Bank's mountain aquifer, one of two major renewable water sources in the territory it seized in a 1967 war.

The other source, the Jordan River dividing the West Bank from Jordan, is dominated by Israel for nearby Jewish farms...

If pupils put themselves in the position of the Khabirat family, how would they feel? What would they do? How could they draw attention to their plight?

Children swimming in the Okavango (supplied)

The water is cool and clean; but unfortunately, it also contains snails which harbour the bilharzia parasite, which causes a dangerous disease. Most children already have these parasites in them, but it does not stop them swimming, as they have no choice – it's hot and the nearest swimming pool is hundreds of kilometres away. Children love water everywhere, so it is doubly important that we try to keep it clean. In the UK, Surfers Against Sewage (SAS) has campaigned for years to prevent sewage being pumped into the sea near bathing beaches, and has had a spectacular influence on what water authorities are allowed to do. Thanks to them, many beaches have been made safe for swimming again.

As well as a source of fun, water remains an important form of communication and transport. Our canals in the UK are now mainly used for pleasure boats and barges, but along the River Rhine for example and even the Thames, and in many parts of the world the waterways are still used to transport huge amounts of cargo. Ferries still carry masses of cargo between the UK and Europe; the Channel between Dover and Calais is the busiest shipping lane in the world. Consequently there is always the risk of accidents and spillages of dangerous substances. Oil spills have ruined beaches and killed wildlife in many parts of the world. Encourage pupils to learn about some of these disasters, or search for information on the internet about organisations that care for seals and birds affected by oil spills. There are seal sanctuaries in Cornwall, Norfolk and Scotland. You can find out more about them on www.sealsanctuary.co.uk.

Partnership, water and eco-literacy

To conclude this chapter, let's draw together the key ideas. Eco-literacy is about understanding how the many networks operate – how pulling strings in one place affects things elsewhere in the net. The water network involves consumers (us), water companies (big business), farmers, environmentalists (like SAS), industries that use water, people who live close to water, government, and all the animals and plants that live in water and depend on it. An outbreak of pollution in one place can have an impact on many others. Inadequate funding for water treatment will affect everyone. Over-extraction of water in one place means a shortage somewhere else. Polluting the atmosphere with too much carbon dioxide could ultimately cause floods and raise sea-levels. Pacific Islands and much of Bangladesh could disappear. Pupils can talk and think about these connections in the web of life, and seek reliable information on which to base their ideas.

Partnership means working together to prevent the kinds of disasters discussed above. We can all make an impact, as SAS has shown. Children in many areas have collected evidence about their local rivers and water supplies which have been valuable in influencing the way farmers and water companies operate. Gaining publicity is often a key element in this, and children are excellent publicisers of environmental problems. They care about fairness, and understand the ethical issues discussed in the previous chapter. Often, if they are listened to, they will go on to be active in environmental organisations or in their local communities. They will pull strings in the local political networks in ways that others cannot. Teachers and parents cannot ignore them, patronise them, imagine they don't understand or laugh at the points they make. During the outbreak of the Iraq war, children in the UK were sometimes punished with detention for missing school to demonstrate, sensibly and powerfully, against the war. As long as teachers suppress children like that, books like this will be a waste of time. As Michael Roth (2003), a Canadian environmental educator, observes:

> Rather than preparing students for life in a technological world, I work with teachers to create opportunities for participating in this world and for learning science in the process of contributing to everyday life of the community... early participation in community-relevant practices provides for continuous participation and a greater relevance of schooling to the everyday life of its main constituents.

Not everyone has to know the same things or be competent in the same fields, on the same issues. What matters is that in partnership, we produce the knowledge and action relevant to the problems at hand.

10

Eco-design

Over the last few years, there have been many programmes on TV about design: Changing Rooms, Ground Force, Grand Designs, and many others. The theme running through all of them is re-designing our environment to make it better; though what better means is not always clear. So a good starting point would be to get your children to think about *making things better* and what it means. For example;

> What would be a better bike? A better packed lunch? A better house? A better school uniform? A better kitchen? A better school toilet? Better cars? Even, a better school?

Children can also think about *making work easier*. Brainstorm the kinds of work they and their parents do, then ask them to suggest how the work could be done to use less energy. For example; drying clothes on the line uses less energy than putting them in the tumble drier. Walking or cycling uses less energy than going by car. Some schools now operate a Virtual Bus which has children walking to school together, picking each other up at bus stops along the way.

Children's views about 'The School I'd Like' have been collected in a new book by Burke and Grosvenor (2003), which shows some excitingly creative ideas. So children can be creative about re-designing things. The question is, do their designs take account of the ecological principles discussed in previous chapters? Let them first try to re-think the design of something simple, before considering more complex things like their homes.

> A good example would be anything in regular use but which might be inefficient, like a kettle, a toilet, a school-bag, a mobile phone.

> • What is it made of, and where?
> • How much energy is used in making it?
> • How could it be made/delivered more cheaply?
> • In what ways is it inefficient?

And most importantly perhaps,

• Do I really need it? What could I use instead?

Eco-design is not just about things like machines and houses but also about our social practices. For example, how often do we use our cars, and is every car journey necessary? What do we do in our spare time, and what are the environmental costs of music, clothes, going to clubs, flying to other countries for holidays? Where would pupils draw the lines between necessity, preference and luxury? They may be familiar with the Three Rs – Reduce, Re-use, Recycle – but little attention is paid to the first of these. Redesigning can also mean finding ways to do without something.

After relating these issues to a familiar subject, pupils will be ready to apply the six principles of eco-literacy discussed at the beginning of this book:

Networks – all living systems are interconnected. What we do affects others.

Cycles – ecosystems that survive produce no net waste.
Waste from one process is food for another.
(Biodynamic farming is a good example of this)

Solar energy – all our energy comes ultimately from the sun.
Photosynthesis drives all living processes.

Partnership – we have to co-operate in designing things that work for us all.

Diversity – ecosystems remain resilient through richness and complexity.
More diversity means greater resistance to attack.

Balance – feedback loops help restore balance. We cannot take too much from a system (e.g. fish from the sea) without imbalancing and endangering it.

Eco-design should ensure that what we do fits in with these principles. It is not about what we can take from nature but what we can learn from nature to ensure sustainability.

For example, there is at present a problem of over-fishing species like cod and haddock in the seas around Europe. Strict quotas have also required fishermen to throw back dead fish because they have caught too many. One design that could solve this is a system of deep-sea fish-farms, based on cages like this:

Does this take account of all six principles? What will be the impact on the sea bed, on the trawler fishing industry in places like Cornwall and the Shetlands, or on other species? New methods of farming salmon or trawling for sea bass have recently created problems of disease and death for other species, problems that were not anticipated.

Recycling is one way in which designs can be ecologically sustainable. Some big companies have introduced systems for recycling most of the materials they use. For example, Canon have redesigned their copiers so that 90% of their components can be recycled. Fiat cars have introduced 300 dismantling centres in which they recycle the steel, plastics, glass, seat padding and many other components of their old cars: 95% will be recycled by 2010.

The aim is to make more from less, by means of good design. The United Nations Environment Programme (UNEP) has initiated its 'Factor Ten Goals', so called because they believe that developed countries like ours could, using existing technologies, reduce raw material use by a factor of ten through re-use and recycling.

Homes and buildings

This is one of the areas where saving on energy and materials can be most effective.

Pupils can consider what could make a difference in the way their house or school is built, so that energy and materials are reduced, for instance the shape and the way it faces; the building materials used; windows; lighting and heating, and insulation. A house can be designed to make the most of the sun and wind if it is in the right position to catch the sun and shelter from the wind. Energy use in a building can thus be cut by about 30%.

Bricks and cement use a great deal of energy in their production: cement manufacture is one of the biggest producers of carbon dioxide on the planet. Wood is cheap to obtain, and is renewable, unlike rock. Recycled timber can be used for most parts of a house. Straw bale houses are also becoming popular, but the biggest increase in eco-friendly housing is in timber-frame self-build housing. Masonite (wooden) beams allow for building bigger rooms using timber frames. There is more about building wooden houses at www. woodforgood.com, info@ segalselfbuild.co.uk or www.buildstore. co.uk

Windows cause the biggest heat loss from a building, at night and in winter. There are now special kinds of glass (low-E glass) that reflect back heat but not light; double- and triple-glazing can be fitted that can be gas-filled to cut down noise and heat loss.

Modern lighting systems using long-life tubes can save up to 90% on electricity costs. Solar photo-voltaic (PV) panels in the roof and walls can generate enough electricity to power the whole house.

Of all the design features of a house, correct insulation saves most energy. When air is confined in small areas, it is an excellent insulator. This is the principle of the string vest. Most types of insulation work by trapping air in a light fabric. The thicker the insulation, the better it works. Polystyrene, straw, newspaper, rockwool and even sheep's wool are now used. Wool has been used to keep people warm for centuries. Some farmers are now rearing sheep exclusively to provide fleece for house insulation. Activities about insulation are described below.

The labour involved in building a house is also renewable, so the best way is to build it using local builders and suppliers, to build partnerships and encourage local industries. A good example is the Eden Project in Cornwall. Every item it uses is obtained locally in Cornwall except one (photographic film), thus benefiting the local economy, and local people's jobs, by over £100 million a year. Such social enterprise means that the community comes together to develop a business that will benefit everyone.

Even if one is not building a new house or school, huge improvements and savings can be made by refitting existing buildings in the ways described. Not only does this save money but it helps minimise energy use and preserve the environment.

Imagine that your house or school is like a tree: it should be able to purify the air entering it, use the sun's heat and light, produce more energy than it uses, create shade and a good habitat for people and plants, enrich not deplete the soil around it, and change with the seasons. Buildings can do this, so how could you change yours, to make it work more like a tree?

The way we live

Sustainable housing is not just about design; it is also about the way we live in our houses. More people are choosing to live singly, without children, so smaller houses are required. More people want a second home in the country; in some areas of Devon, Cornwall and the Lake District, over half the houses are now second homes, lived in only on weekends and holidays. This has an impact on the sustainability of shops, post offices, garages, newsagents and other small businesses. Local people on low incomes cannot afford to buy homes in their own town, creating social unrest and more movement out of rural areas. Local public transport suffers, since the weekenders use their own vehicles.

This is a good topic for pupils to study in depth. Set pupils the task of designing small houses suitable for local people on low incomes. They can find out about the cheapest, low-energy ways of building, and about matters like planning permission and the price of land. For example; sloping land is expensive to level for foundations, so it is usually cheaper than flat land. However, post and beam houses can just as easily be built on a slope, so saving money. They can also do simple surveys among local people about what kind of houses they prefer.

Activities related to insulation and ventilation

There are many valuable science skills to be learned from doing fair tests on insulating materials. Using sensing and data-logging equipment enhances such activities. A simple way to determine effectiveness is to set out containers of hot water, leaving one open to the elements, while insulating the others using different materials.

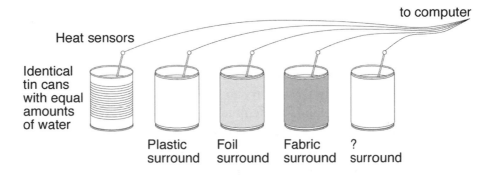

Drawing of how to set up insulation tests

The first test would use the same thickness of different insulating materials, such as rockwool, shredded newspaper, straw, sheep's wool. Samples of all these can be obtained from builders' merchants. The sensors will indicate the fall in temperature when insulated and when not, showing which material is best.

A second test could use different thicknesses of the same insulator. This will show pupils how increasing the thickness helps reduce the amount of heating needed in a house. They can find out about cavity-wall insulation, 'breathing walls', double-glazing and other ways that builders save energy.

Visiting a building site can be difficult to organise for health and safety reasons, so it's easier to invite a builder to school. Most builders will have samples to illustrate building techniques to children. Video clips from TV series such as Grand Designs illustrate precisely how houses are built to save energy. Building instructors at a nearby FE college may also be willing to meet with primary classes.

Pupils may not understand how heat is lost from a house if all the doors and windows are shut. A simple way to illustrate this is to inflate a model house or doll's house, blowing air into the house with a bicycle pump. They will be able to feel where air is escaping. Connecting the pump to an old torn football or balloon placed inside the house will make this easier. All new houses will soon have to be pressure tested by buildings inspectors in this way. The children will soon see that heated air escapes through the roof, around all the windows and doors, through air vents and floors.

A house that is perfectly sealed to prevent air escaping would be very unhealthy to live in, however, and bad for the house, causing condensation and damp. So ventilation is needed.

> Pupils can search their own homes to find where the air gets in: all houses must have ventilation bricks, and these should be open. They can also find out where there are extractor fans, which windows open, and how air flows through the house, by lighting candles with doors and windows open, and watching how the smoke moves. Could they design better windows? Which ones are best for ventilation and insulation?

Access and security: the triple bottom line

House prices keep rising in this country and the most cheaply built house may not always be best. Other things matter, such as having easy access for old and disabled people and security to prevent people breaking in.

A brainstorm by the class about how they could test a house for security and access would produce items like these:

- Could someone get into the house on their own in a wheelchair?

- Could they get upstairs, or into a bathroom?

- What kind of door locks are used?

- Do the windows lock?

- Is the outside of the house well lit?

- Is the house alarmed?

- Has it been burgled before?

They can then examine their school and their own homes to see how well they score.

Exploring this issue provides an opportunity to link the science and design aspects of housing with citizenship ideas relating to community. Our community is unlikely to survive if we all do our own thing, such as throwing rubbish into the street, playing loud music all night, parking cars where they block access, vandalising, fighting and bullying, and generally being anti-social. Communities often rely on the law to regulate anti-social behaviour, but this isn't always realistic when the nearest policeman is many miles away.

Pupils could find out what Neighbourhood Watch organisations do, and someone who represents a local scheme might come to speak to the school. Pupils could ask them about the sustainability of their work: who is involved in the network? Who keeps it going? How is feedback provided? How are different views represented to come to a balanced conclusion? Does it make a difference?

Living with our neighbours

Successful ecosystems are those which survive. This is a simple idea, but not so simple to create. If a village or an estate or a street is to survive, people have to get on with each other. What do we need of our community if it is to survive in harmony?

In this consideration of human rights or citizens' rights issues, children may not realise how fortunate they are compared with their peers in many other countries. Two good reference books are *Who Decides?* (Price, 2001), which has many activities that link to work on community and conflict and *Children as Citizens* by Holden and Clough (1998). Both focus on children's thinking on what it means to be an active citizen.

All these activities link to the underlying question throughout the book: *Who Decides?*

For example, who decides
- whether or not we walk to school?
- to provide cycle routes?
- how our classrooms are designed?
- whether we have kerbside collections for recycling?
- where the recycling banks are located?
- where new houses are built?
- that the local post office be closed down?

One of the activities used is the familiar technique of Mind Mapping. Pupils create a mind map relating to ideas such as 'home', 'community', or 'conflict', using green for positive notions and red for negative ones. Or make an Outcome Tree relating to one of the ideas raised – see below.

Effects

Solutions

What happened?

Causes

Clothing and fashion

Eco-design can link to children's interests in fashion. What do pupils know and believe? Ask them questions such as:

> What are your clothes made of?
> Which are made from natural materials (e.g. cotton, wool, linen, leather, fur)?
> Which are made from artificial fibres (e.g. nylon, lycra, polyester, neoprene)?
> What are these artificial fibres made from? (petroleum products)
> Where are your clothes made? (mostly in developing countries)
> Who makes them? (mostly poorly-paid women and children)
> How many shirts/tops/coats/shoes do you have?
> Why do people buy new clothes so often? Why do fashions change?
> Which are the main clothing shops they buy from?
> How much would you ask your parents to pay for a pair of jeans/ a top/a pair of shoes?

Children and adults often buy clothing without knowing the full implications of their choices. Yet there are issues of sustainability arising from choices of materials, where they are made, which company you buy from, and how much you pay.

Materials

Ask pupils to make one list of the natural materials used in clothing and another of the artificial materials. The most common natural materials are cotton, wool, linen, leather and fur. They can look at the tags in each other's shirts, shoes and trousers. Some materials are difficult to classify (such as Nu-buck in shoes) and require web-based research.

Next, find out where and how these materials are produced. Pupils will know that wool comes from sheep, leather from cows and calves, but they may know less about how fur and linen are produced. Mink farming for furs in the UK has led to the escape of 'wild' mink that have seriously affected the ecology of some areas, as the mink destroy other small mammal populations. Seal culling in Canada has set off major campaigns against the killing of wild animals for fur. Many strict vegetarians will not wear leather shoes.

Pupils may know that cotton is grown on small bushes, but not where it is grown, or that the slave trade was driven by the need for cheap labour on the cotton plantations in the United States. The key issue is cost; if we had to pay the fair trade price for cotton, how much would our clothes cost?

What makes up the cost of a pair of jeans?

Before someone from a clothing shop comes to talk to them, pupils should estimate the cost of each aspect. They will know how much a pair of jeans costs;

ask them to discuss how much they think goes on the raw materials, wages of workers, energy, warehousing, transport, wholesalers' profit, retailers' profit. They will be surprised to find out how little goes on raw materials and workers' wages!

The dilemma over GM cotton

Cotton, from which jeans are made, is now being genetically modified to make the cotton plant resistant to parasites and diseases. Is this good or bad? There are arguments on both sides, as always. More resistant cotton means more reliable crops, bigger yields, so that small farmers can produce more and sell more. But the GM cotton seeds are produced by multinational agrochemical companies, so small farmers are dependent on buying from them, and the big companies control the price. Also, a rise in the yield of cotton produces a glut on the world market, lowering the price the growers receive. Big countries solve this by sub-sidising their growers, guaranteeing them a minimum price and setting up trade barriers against growers from poorer countries who can produce cotton more cheaply. Hence the poor farmers in the developing world lose their markets and can't sell their cotton.

Pupils can find out more about these issues by searching the Planetark website, www.planetark.org To discuss the issues in a simulation exercise, they can take on the following roles:

GM cotton seed manufacturer (USA)
Clothing manufacturer in Indonesia
Cotton grower in India
Clothing factory worker in Indonesia
High street retailer (e.g. GAP)
Customer

They can each take a position based on their findings from the news items on the website. When each has put their case, the class can decide what should be done, and determine a fair price for a pair of jeans. With their new knowledge, they can research jeans in the various high street stores, in terms of price, where they are made, whether the label indicates that they are made from GM cotton, and so on.

In India, local scientists have produced a pirate GM cotton seed independently of the multinationals and are selling it more cheaply to farmers, who like it better. This is also worth discussing – will it help farmers in the long run, and in what way? Will it lead to a more sustainable cotton industry in India? Who benefits? What will the big companies do?

How changing fashions affect other aspects of life

The widespread introduction of nylon and rayon in the 1950s led to a revolution in clothing design and manufacture, and this in turn strongly affected the cotton weaving industry in Britain. Most cotton mills in Lancashire suffered from the fashion for nylon and the importing of cheaper 'Indian cotton' products from India and Pakistan. Some went over to weaving nylon and polyester or changed to specialist weaving and dyeing, but most closed down. In Lancashire and areas such as Bradford and Leicester, there had been a huge influx of workers from the developing world to work in the clothing trade. Your grandparents who worked in weaving or manufacturing might be able to come to school to talk about the changes.

With immigration came the racist attitudes of some people who saw the immigrants as taking their jobs. The residual hostility is still evident in the election of BNP councillors in northern textile towns such as Burnley, Blackburn and Halifax, and the tabloid press makes much of stories about racial conflict. However, the reasons communities are in conflict are highly complex and pupils should have any stereotypical assumptions challenged. The sustainability of an industry is also affected by social and political issues.

On the sensitive issue of asylum-seekers the right questions must be asked:

- Why are people leaving their own country, at great risk and expense?
- Why are they choosing to come to Britain?
- What do the asylum seekers themselves say about this?
- What is the difference between an asylum seeker and an economic migrant?
- What skills do recent immigrants have?
- Should they be allowed to work?
- What lessons can be learned from the drownings in Morecambe Bay?

There are currently severe shortages of, for instance, builders, plumbers, fruit and flower pickers, nurses and teachers in many areas of Britain. Why might this be, and should we encourage immigrants (e.g. from countries like Poland that have now joined the EU) to do this work?

Thus the debate ranges over diverse issues. When pupils apply their eco-literacy skills to the issue of fashion design they might consider issues of:

partnership – are people being treated fairly or exploited?

networks – do we communicate with each other and discuss things, or do we (and the fashion industry) assume we know what is good for people?

bio-diversity – could growing more GM cotton be threatening the natural crop?

the triple bottom line – what would our clothes cost if everyone involved in the clothing industry considered the social and environmental costs?

responsible eco-design – are we buying and demanding clothing from companies who have these interests at heart, or do we not care who makes our clothes, as long as they are cheap?

Lessons: the role of 'political teacher' in promoting eco-design

In *Education for the Future*, Dave Hicks (2002) writes:

> The Celtic peoples insisted that only poets could be teachers. Why? I think it is because knowledge that is not passed through the heart is dangerous; it may lack wisdom...

The ideas in this chapter may seem ambitious for children of primary age. Their relevance to the basics may not be apparent, and they may seem to take up much classroom time. There is some truth in these concerns. Consequently teachers need to show particular courage and wisdom in judging the issues of eco-literacy and eco-design to commit to in class. The pupils will certainly rise to the challenge. They will see the point, enjoy the work and welcome this approach.

Any resistance is more likely to come from parents and colleagues. Because addressing these issues is being political. The issues to do with who decides, how much workers are paid, which cotton is used, whether fur is fashionable, are issues of power and resources, and anything that involves power and resources is political.

Yet even the question of how money is spent in your school is political and pupils as well as teachers have strong views about it. Ask them about school toilets and school lunches, and the political dimension will soon be apparent. Being political is part of the teaching and learning process. What parents worry about is that teachers might impose some party political views on their children. So it is best to openly acknowledge the political nature of what pupils are doing, thinking and learning and distinguish it clearly from parliamentary arguments about hospitals, education, etc.

Eco-literacy is not about taking sides; it is about understanding the implications of our actions for other people in the worldwide web of interdependence. Every time we buy a shirt, throw rubbish in the bin, ride in a car, buy a CD, eat a burger, we are making a choice that has implications for others. The teacher can teach in a way that makes pupils think about their actions. Letting pupils watch huge trucks tipping *their* rubbish into a landfill site makes an impact. Holding the kilo bag of sugar that represents the greenhouse gas from just one school run makes an impact. Listening to a sheep farmer, a clothing worker, a fisherman or the manager of Top Shop talk about their jobs makes an impact. Thinking, talking and acting on these matters is developing eco-literacy. And it is a vital part of the curriculum for the pupils' future.

11

Making eco-literacy work in
the primary school

This final chapter tries to respond to the thought that follows so many apparently idealistic or radical initiatives in teaching: 'it's a great idea but...' or 'it won't work here because...'. I hope it will help move readers beyond the tipping-point into action. Can you really turn a good idea into actuality in your school? This chapter shows you how it can be done.

Convincing others

Most importantly, the headteacher must be on your side. Very few initiatives thrive without their support. If she is already sympathetic skip this section. If not, try a few of these ideas.

- If you are a trainee applying for your first job, or you are thinking of changing schools, ask at interview about their views on an eco-dimension to the curriculum. You might suggest things you would like to do and gauge their response. It is always more difficult to succeed in a school that doesn't share your values.

- Invite people in who will bring eco-resources and skills into your school, to work with pupils, preferably without cost. Many trusts now have outreach teams that are visiting schools, such as the Somerset Waste Action team or Wildlife trusts. Their specialist knowledge is much valued by children, and the opportunities they present for both publicity and community links are often effective in convincing headteachers that something worthwhile is developing.

- Develop a partnership link with your nearest Initial Teacher Training (ITT) university or college. This can lead to a variety of opportunities – for instance having specialist students on placement, meeting other teachers with similar interests, and joint school-university activities. Being a partner school gives access to a wider range of ideas, materials, like-minded teachers, specialists and activities to bolster your programmes.

- Engage pupils in eco-literate art work that has high visibility, along the lines of such artists as Andy Goldsworthy and Chris Drury.

- Involve parents who have skills and access to resources or environmental sites of interest. Bring them in to work with you in science, art, drama, geography or citizenship sessions.

- Use local Theatre in Education (TiE) groups who offer role-play and simulation activities on eco-themes, such as the Stepping Stones company from Derby University.

- These are all examples of how you are part of different networks. Eco-literacy is about understanding how networks operate, so find out which buttons to press to move things forward. Sowing the seed of a new idea in someone else's head can have ramifications far beyond those you might envisage, as they are likely to be part of other networks that can help you. The idea of 'Six Degrees of Separation' reminds us how close we are to apparent strangers.

- Use all your networks to create and disseminate a display of eco-literacy work done by pupils, to show how effective a change of emphasis can be.

- Be patient. Best not to alienate those who will be needed as allies. Don't cut off your supply lines, and don't let your enthusiasm run away with you.

Finding room for eco-literacy within the timetable

This can seem a daunting hurdle to overcome but there are many ways of organising the weekly programme for the class and many ways of changing it. First list what you see as the obstacles to change: is it the headteacher, colleagues (all, or one or two powerful people?), parents, resources, time?

Change is about strategy: do you opt for revolution, or evolution? You may have the energy, creativity and drive to develop a new idea that will sweep away the old and replace it, or you may be the softly-softly type who works in the background, gradually persuading people at meetings and demonstrating successful change in your classroom. Analyse the opposition and develop a strategy you can communicate clearly and consistently.

It helps to have the children on your side. Some of your science, art, geography, citizenship or literacy sessions would have developed their interest and support for a different way of organising their work. This makes a powerful case, especially if pupils are doing well in the assessed subjects as a consequence of renewed interest and enthusiasm for learning. There is evidence to show that when children are using all the soft skills, rather than just learning mechanically, attainment in the basic skills increases. I saw this when working closely with a teacher in rural Kenya who abandoned the curriculum and organised all the children's work round solving problems the community faced. Instead of formal language or maths lessons, his class worked on how to tackle local illnesses, the problem of traffic in the market, keeping and harvesting fish, building a windmill big enough to saw logs of wood, making furniture and much else. At the end of primary school, his class scored the highest marks in the district in the English, Maths and Science tests. Why? Because they were committed, they tangled with everyday concerns in their community, they talked and discussed and worked things out collaboratively, drawing on local expertise. Just the way children work best in order to become eco-literate.

Once the pupils are on your side and there is evidence of effectiveness and external resource support, you are in a strong position. If you have an inspection coming up, encourage the inspectors to see, and maybe get involved in, your eco-work. Inspectors have frequently praised teachers and schools for work done in the environment and the way it has enhanced pupils' enthusiasm and literacy development.

Modelling good curriculum practice to colleagues

The next thing to decide is how flexible the timetable needs to be in your year. Are the other teachers in your year group willing to work in a similar way? Will you still have to devote the morning to literacy and numeracy, or can you have one day to devote to environmental work or activities outside the classroom? If you only have flexibility in the afternoons, what is feasible? If your innovative developments are successful and popular, you will gradually gain leeway to make more changes. Sound people out. You need at least 40% of your colleagues behind you, if change is to last.

The curriculum is not synonymous with timetable; it is about what we want children to experience. Even within a tight framework of subject teaching, what goes on within literacy or other subjects can be manipulated to achieve several outcomes. For example, much of the reading, researching, discussing and idea-generation suggested in this book can take place in language lessons, some of them focused on topical eco-issues. There is no shortage of literature, drama and poetry that tackles these matters head on for children. For example, *The Stream* by Brian Clarke (2000) is an accessible novel about pollution and conservation, which looks at it from all sides. Ever since John Clare, poets have tackled environmental issues like destruction of habitats and the enclosure of common land. Clare's poems could be an excellent starting point for children to consider the impact of their own actions – and reading them is not just about literacy. Pupils will be learning in other subjects, particularly science, geography and citizenship. Think of eco-literacy as a net that catches many different curricular fish.

Having a clear rationale

When you are asked 'Why is eco-literacy the most effective way of integrating the curriculum?' you need to have an answer. This book may have helped but you still need to work out a personal rationale related to your school, community, and your own world-view. I hate the term 'mission statement', but it helps to put down in writing exactly what it is you're trying to do, so you can speak convincingly whenever called on to make a case for change.

Thinking about your rationale – or getting pupils to do so – will be helped by tackling the word search below. This is not a conventional word search as the words are all given. What you have to do is to articulate *your* idea of how any pair of words is connected.

The word search is organised round the four elements of life – earth, air, fire, water. The words chosen are all superficially like these – some are anagrams and some homophones – but they have very different meanings; so what is the connection, for example, between 'earth' and its anagram 'Heart'? The propositions and ideas you come up with will help you clarify your philosophy of eco-literacy. Your rationale for focusing on eco-literacy must have a hard edge: why, how, what it will achieve.

Another approach is via a SWOT analysis: listing the strengths, weaknesses, opportunities and threats in your proposal. You are right to focus on your strengths and opportunities but need to pay attention to weaknesses and threats, so that you have a strategy for dealing with them. The SWOT analysis begun below can be continued.

Strengths	Weaknesses	Opportunities	Threats
Increased relevance of my teaching to 'real world' issues for children in 21st century	May not show clearly how core subjects are being taught to standards	To make links with external organisations and environmental centres for off-site work	Opposition from colleagues who fear lowered test results

Acting responsibly

To convince others that you want to do all you can towards creating a sustainable future for life on the planet, you will have to lead by example. It is no good setting up compost bins in school and throwing your own apple cores in with the plastic, nor coming away from the supermarket carrying a dozen plastic bags nor buying organic food but not recycled paper. It is easy to be inconsistent, so admit any unsustainable practices. But discuss with pupils how to get round the problems. For example, you welcome cheap flights but realise that aircraft are a major source of pollution, so what do you do when it comes to holidays abroad? There is a whole class topic in that simple idea.

Some decisions are simpler. We don't have to buy green beans and sugar snap peas that have been flown 5,000 miles, nor do we have to use disposable cameras and razors. You could do an inventory of your plus and minus practices, and resolve to break another unsustainable habit each year, modelling reflection on your practices to your pupils and colleagues. You could measure how much waste the school produces and compare it with a similar-sized school nearby to see how well it is doing.

Using the environment to develop eco-literacy

This is a powerful way of making a case to colleagues, parents and children. Many books offer excellent ideas, such as Joseph Cornell's *Sharing Nature with Children* (1989) and Steve van Matre's *Earth Education* (1990). Local groups and organisations are willing to help with ideas that work locally, such as the National Trust, National Park wardens, and the British Trust for Conservation Volunteers. The National Foundation for Educational Research also has its Environmental Education Research Network (FERN) that can put you in touch with ideas and organisations, such as FACE (Farming and Countryside Educa-tion).

Begin with the school environment, collecting rainwater, putting in worm bins and composters, planting trees, making havens for wildlife. These are visible signs of being concerned and informed about eco-issues. Pupils can do research into the way their environment is changing: water levels, pond life, development of weeds, daisies, dandelions ... One small school in Cornwall discovered that their new pond became colonised by frogs and toads and that when they reproduced and migrated, the frogs went one way and the toads the other. Why was this? A real research study was conducted, based on their own observations. And schools can carry out longitudinal studies over several years, data being collected by new pupils each year.

Work of this kind can be expanded by using trusts, national parks and environmental centres which exist in most areas of the country, including city centres. The National Trust Guardianship Scheme now links over 100 schools to National Trust properties across the country (see chapter 8 for website address). Children take responsibility for some aspect of maintaining the grounds, and visit around six times a year to carry out work such as clearing bracken, putting up bird-boxes, planting trees, and doing small-scale research. The scheme is sponsored by Norwich Union and has few if any cost implications for the schools. Children make strong attachments to 'their' land, and learn to act responsibly in relation to the environment. They see the wardens as knowledgeable, caring role-models and are influenced by them.

Schools can also visit purpose-built centres such as the Eden Project, the Earth Centre, The Living Rainforest, Magna, and many others. All provide first-hand experiences which have huge impact on children and continue to influence their thinking. It often works out cheaper to make trips with small (half a class) groups in self-drive minibuses rather than hiring a coach. Centre websites provide virtual tours and ideas for activities that can be done without visiting. For web addresses see page 118.

Another disadvantage to a coach trip is that it may be seen as a day out rather than a learning experience. To help children focus on what you want them to experience you need to have

- *prepared effectively*, so that pupils know what the day is for, and have clear expectations about what they are going to see and do

- *good organisation*, so that no time is wasted by late arrivals, toilet trips, cumbersome clipboards, lost pencils, bags that are too heavy, inappropriate clothing etc.

- *mediation* by adults who know how to encourage children's learning, especially by good questioning. A ratio of 1:4 is needed if children are really going to learn. Most centres let accompanying adults in free with school trips, so encourage parents to come. It is also good education for them, and reinforces school-community links.

- *to avoid death by worksheet.* At a place as stunning as the Eden Project, it is sad to see children with their heads down in a worksheet, running from place to place to tick things off. The experience is what counts. Written work is best done back in school, when children can download many of the activity sheets themselves from websites. And this saves paper.

- *time to stop, gather and talk.* Children need to ask, to make sense of what they are doing, rather than to be swept along from one new sensory experience to another. Talk is much more valuable, and less time-consuming, than writing or drawing. They can use a digital camera or a minidisk recorder if they need a record for later.

Strengthening your case through working with the community

When trying to develop eco-literacy, take cues for thinking, knowing and learning from everyday community-based interaction, where ideas are talked about and contested. Real, worthwhile eco-literacy may only emerge from collective effort involving all the community. It goes on in all kinds of places – pubs, bus-stops, shops, youth clubs, parish councils.

Any kind of literacy, including eco-literacy, is not only about what is said but also about the struggle to get something said (and heard) in the first place. Making one's voice heard is part of literacy, as is gaining access to conversations, and avoiding being patronised. Children need to learn these skills too.

Thus developing eco-literacy is a collective social enterprise. It develops when specialist professionals and ordinary people with different backgrounds engage each other over contentious and personally relevant issues, and gradually involve children as they mature. The optimal context will be an active community which offers possibilities for things to happen, and which values all its members, including children.

Working with your community is a bit like weaving cloth. Your own specialist eco-knowledge, and that of other local experts, is the warp: other knowledge, concerns and ideas from within your community makes up the threads or weft. Interest, concern, new ideas, commitment and action are woven from their interaction. And you are the weaver. In the words of Michael Roth (2003):

> If we take scientific literacy to be a characteristic of emergent collective practice, then it does not matter which piece each and everyone contributes but that, in the end, decisions are made that take account of a variety of relevant (local) knowledge, values and beliefs.

In other words, learning no longer belongs to individual persons but to the various conversations of which they are part. Not everyone has to know the same things or be competent on the same issues. We cannot all know enough to make informed decisions about everything. What matters is that as a community you produce the knowledge relevant to the problems at hand. Children have a place in this and are not merely recipients of other people's wisdom.

Children can, for example participate in activities that benefit their community, and contribute to debates about matters that are relevant to them, their parents and their community at large. Why don't we have a paper recycling facility in our school? Why do we have to drive ten miles to recycle our glass? Where would be a good place for a wind farm? At the moment, for example, a campaign is being publicised to persuade fast food outlets such as Macdonalds to take responsibility for clearing up the litter produced by customers disposing of their containers. Where do children stand on this? How could they be involved actively?

Instead of preparing children for life in someone else's future technological world, think of working to create opportunities for them to participate more actively in this world. Eco-literacy means learning the process of contributing to the everyday life of the community, and participation in community-relevant practices from an early age makes schooling more relevant for the everyday life of your children. Identifying with their own local issues from an early age makes children feel responsible and proud of what they have achieved. Ask teachers of infants who have been part of any recycling campaign. They will tell you how good these infants are at policing teachers' and parents' waste disposal habits!

Local initiatives
Supporting local initiatives is a good way to strengthen community networks and gain support for the work in school. Become involved in waste minimisation, recycling and wildlife conservation. Local councils, voluntary organisations, youth groups, women's institutes and the like will be engaged in activities the school can make links with. The children can pass on ideas and information gleaned from their research and contribute their youthful energy.

Linking with schools in the developing world
Water, sanitation, pollution, conservation, deforestation, HIV/AIDS, food production, energy generation and climate change are important issues everywhere, but they affect people in poor countries more severely. Knowing how children elsewhere are affected can spur pupils to act. Links can be established with schools in the developing world. Organisations like the United Kingdom One World Linking Association, for example, (www.ukowla.org.uk) offer schools guidance on how to search for a partner. Link Africa (www.link africa.org)

enables UK schools to link up with schools in South Africa, Ghana, Kenya and elsewhere, and provides opportunities for teachers to visit schools in these countries. Neighbouring schools may already have such links and certain local authorities have developed links with specific countries for exchange purposes. There is no better way of seeing your own system in a new light than by seeing it through the eyes of children from another culture. Education staff from Oxfam or similar non-governmental aid agencies can help the school get started and provide relevant resources.

The political dimension of this linking – who decides? who gets what? – relates to citizenship and interests children. When aid was diverted to Iraq from other needy countries in 2003, for example, this would be of concern to children who have forged links with poor countries in Africa. What will be the impact on the ecologies and economies of those whose aid budget is cut? Why are the poorest countries always the worst affected?

Focusing on the topical

Children have a strong sense of fairness and will want to talk about some of these eco-issues in light of the injustices they see. Teachers shouldn't be reluctant to tackle such matters as:

- **Need and greed** – What do we really need, and what is simply greed? Pupils can think about this in relation to everyday things like food, clothing, household appliances, make-up, leisure activities, then relate them to what children 'need' in other countries. Why should we be different?

- **Money** – Why does it always come down to money? Who has all the money, where does it come from, who decides what it gets spent on? Why do some people get paid so much more than others? A young graduate in a London law firm earns over £35,000 a year whereas the – much older – cleaners in her office get less than a quarter of that. Why? Is it fair?

- **Who makes the big decisions? Who is responsible?** Is it politicians, businessmen, celebrities, the media? Or is it actually us? Focus on a local issue that has been controversial, and find out how decisions got made, who ultimately had their way. Why is this? What could we have done? Why do people not act?

- **Are we safe?** What is likely to happen if the world heats up, if terrorism spreads, if we clone babies, if we eat GM foods? Do we know what the risk is? The media carry scare stories about such things, but seldom about the dangers of earthquakes, smoking, crossing the road, cycling, drinking alcohol, taking drugs, eating a bad diet. Teachers will not have the answers, but should nonetheless develop children's eco-literacy by encouraging them to keep asking questions and trying to find out relevant information. To take one example, over a hundred times more deaths each year are caused by water sports than by boxing, so should we ban water sports?

• **What do we want to hang on to? What are we in danger of losing? Why?** Some things change so slowly that we don't realise they are changing and by the time we do, it may be too late. This applies to climate change. Different scientists are predicting different futures. According to one theory, Britain is going to get warmer – and this is already happening. Varieties of birds, fish and plants that used to live further south, such as egrets and red mullet, have migrated to our shores. According to the other, if the arctic icecap keeps melting and the cold North Atlantic currents push the more saline Gulf Stream back, the seas round our coast might freeze in winter and generate a climate like that of Montreal in Eastern Canada. If we want to slow down such changes we have to take action. Do we want cheap coffee, with all the implications for poor farmers in the third world? Or do we want a fairer society, in which case we will have to pay more for our staple foods? Do we want to go on eating cod and chips until all the cod are extinct? What are the alternatives?

Where does this leave us?

This book has tried to make the case that teachers can make a difference to the big ecological issues and so can their pupils. Remember triple bottom line: the cost of anything is not only financial but social and environmental, and that if we don't pay the full price, we are cheating our children out of their future on the planet. Children in Britain seldom realise that they are part of a tiny minority of privileged people. Developing their eco-literacy should help them to see that their privileges should carry obligations. We are all part of one worldwide web and the future is in our children's hands.

Sustainability may appear to be a difficult concept for young children but the notion of using without using up can be made an everyday reality in many ways. We have so much paper, so many pencils, so much spending money; how can we make sure we don't use them up before we can generate more? What can we do to actively generate more? I once worked in a school in Botswana where the teachers cut every pencil into six to make them go further and each pupil had to make their tiny pencil last a term. They sharpened them very carefully!

The message can be summed up as the six Rs: the first three are familiar:

reduce the amount of waste we unthinkingly produce
re-use things instead of throwing them away
recycle materials wherever possible.

Possibly even more important for teachers:

> rethink what you are doing in the classroom and outside it, in your own life
> revise the way you work with pupils
> re-educate colleagues and others by example.

Let's end with a seventh R:

> refuse to be discouraged and diverted by people who are cynical, who simply can't be bothered, who like to toe the line, or who take the easy way. You *can* make a difference.

References

Alexander, R. (2000) *Culture and Pedagogy: International comparisons in primary education.* Oxford: Blackwell.

Association for Science Education (ASE) (2004) Creativity and Science Education (whole issue). *Primary Science Review* 81.

Boyle, G. (1996) *Renewable Energy: Power for a sustainable future.* Oxford: Open University Press, in association with the Open University.

Burke, C. and Grosvenor, I. (2003) *The School I'd Like: Children and young people's reflections on an education for the 21st century.* London: RoutledgeFalmer.

Capra, F. (1996) *The Web of Life: A new synthesis of mind and matter.* London: Harper-Collins.

Capra, F. (2002) *The Hidden Connections: A science for sustainable living.* London: Harper Collins.

Clegg, A.B. (Ed.) (1965) *The Excitement of Writing.* London: Chatto & Windus.

Darvill, P. (2000) *Sir Alec Clegg: A biographical study.* Knebworth: Able Publishing.

Hellden, G. (2003) Personal context and continuity of human thought as recurrent themes in a longitudinal study. *Scandinavian Journal of Educational Research* 47 (2), 205-217.

Hicks, D. (2002) *Lessons for the Future: The missing dimension in education.* London: RoutledgeFalmer.

McGaugh, J.L. (2003) *Memory and Emotion.* London: Weidenfeld.

Price, J. (Ed.) (2001) *Who Decides? Citizenship through Geography.* London: ActionAid .

Roth, M (2003) Scientific literacy as an emergent feature of collective human praxis. *Journal of Curriculum Studies* 35 (1), 9-23.

Steele, T. (1975) *The Life and Death of St. Kilda: The moving story of a vanished island community.* London: Fontana/Collins.

Tudge, C. (2000) *The Variety of Life: A survey and a celebration of all the creatures that have ever lived.* Oxford: Oxford University Press.

Unilever (2000) *Water* (Unilever Educational Booklet, Advanced Series). London: Unilever

Zukav, G. (1979) *The Dancing Wu Li Masters: An overview of the new Physics.* London: Fontana paperbacks.

Websites

www.bbc.co.uk/science/horizon/2003/easterisland.shtml
www.nc.uk.net/usd
www.ecoliteracy.org/pages/foodsystemsproject.html
www.eco-schools.org.uk
www.planetark.org
www.carymoor.org.uk
www.wastewatch.org.uk
www.worldwatch.org
www.norfolkbroads.com/pdf/albatross.pdf
Botanical gardens/Environmental Centres:

www.rbgkew.org.uk	(Kew, London)
www.rbge.org.uk	(Edinburgh)
www.edenproject.com	(Eden Project)
www.bbgardens.org	(Birmingham)
www.anbg.gov.au/anbg	(Australia)
www.ville.montreal.qc.ca/jardin	(Montreal, Canada)
www.htbg.com	(Hawaii)
www.flbg.org	(Florida)

www.devonwildlifetrust.org.
www.unaids.org
www.foodandfarming.org.
www.nationaltrust.org.uk/learninganddiscovery/learning/guardianship/
www.who.int/emc-hiv/fact_sheets/index.html
www.who.int/inf-fs/en/fact109.html
www.zeri.org
www.planetark.org/dailynewsstory.cfm?newsid=18573
www.planetark.org/dailynewsstory.cfm?newsid=21731.
www.sealsanctuary.co.uk
www.woodfrogood.com, info@segalselfbuild.co.uk
www.buildstore.co.uk

INDEX